DYSTOPIA/UTOPIA

THE INFORMATION EDITOR

MILES HUNT

ARCADIA
www.scholarly.info

First Published by Arcadia in 2021
the general books' imprint of
Australian Scholarly Publishing Pty Ltd
7 Lt Lothian St Nth, North Melbourne, VIC 3051
Te: 03 9329 6963
contact@scholarly.info / www.scholarly.info

ISBN: 978-1-7637888-2-4

First published in Australia 2021
This edition published 2025

Typesetting: WorkingType (www.workingtype.com.au)

ACKNOWLEDGEMENTS

Thanks to everyone who contributed to this book. Over the years, there have been so many people, ideas and conversations that have helped inspire the story.

I would not have been able to write this novel without the love and support of my partner, family and friends – all are probably a bit sick of hearing me read little snippets to them whenever I got the chance. But cheers for putting up with me during the bleakest moments.

Thanks so much to New Authors Collective for being part of the journey – any book needs a team and they were mine. Special thanks to my agent, Michael Cybulski, for always believing and never giving up hope; and to Sue Anderson, for giving voice to the underground and making the story so much richer. Also huge thanks to Stephen Pollock for working with the words, reminding me to get to the point and having a profound effect on my writing in general. And Liani Solari, who edited the work and gave it consistency – and helped give the book the ending it deserved.

Thanks also to Luke Heilbuth, Ken Ward, Michael Rakusin, Elissandra Munhoz, Tony Hunt, and Stella Hunt. All have read the book and provided really useful advice and suggestion, whilst giving me the confidence to keep going with this dystopian vision. Not forgetting my sister, Britt Hunt, for finally coming up with a title.

Thanks so much to designer, Simon Greiner, for the incredible cover – it is a work of pop-art in its own right. And Luke Harris at Working Type for helping with the latest version of the cover and novel.

Finally thanks to Nick Walker, Anna Nechkina and everyone at Australian Scholarly Publishing. Nick, I owe you so much gratitude for always supporting my work and getting it out there for people to read – which is of course the point of any novel.

PART I

1.

He stands at the corner, waiting. He looks up and down both streets, searching for a sign of the white van. It is nowhere to be seen. He double-checks the corner to make sure he's standing in the right place. He is. Timewise, it can't be far off.

A wasp suddenly drops out of the sky and hovers close by. It spins around and trains its camera on his face, checking him against its facial recognition database. Could it have recognised him? He knows he may already be on a State watchlist after what he has done, after what they did. He stands, unable to move, not daring to. His hands and legs tremble with fear. The wasp is going to shoot him with a mini missile, he knows it. He can sense it lining him up in its sights, ready to release its most deadly weapon and blow him and half the pavement away. This is his end. But then it flies off, darting down an alley in search of other prey.

He lets out a long, slow breath. He is in danger, he knows it. And things are only going to get worse. After what he has done, everyone is after him: Gorilla Industries, the Home Security Office, everyone. Anywhere he goes, he will be in danger. There are cameras everywhere, looking for his face, and if they spot him, the Company soldiers will descend, a marauding horde of yellow and brown. He can feel the world closing in. *All this for her?*

He hears the low hum of an electric engine. The white van is heading towards him. It is one block away, driving slowly.

He peers down the street, trying to get a glimpse inside. The windscreen is tinted. No light shines through. Parks must be in there, he thinks. He raises a hand, gives a half-wave. Then he realises it's probably driverless. She must be waiting to let him in the back.

The van slows. It approaches him carefully, comes right alongside, as if making sure it is him, and him alone. As it edges past, he moves forward and gets ready to jump in the back, waiting for Parks to open the door.

It is still inching away when the rear doors fly open. Four State Police soldiers jump out. They are puffed up with their thick bulletproof vests; covered from helmet to boot in midnight blue – and they come for him, surging like a dark wave.

He screams out. Panic overwhelms him. He barely moves. Within seconds, he is wrenched to the ground and a brutal, heavy knee slams into his back. They rip his bag from him and chuck it away. It contains the last of his possessions – some clothes, Pep-Me-Up pills and a standard issue Gorilla Industries cap. There is nothing else left from a decade of tireless, thankless work.

"Do NOT move or we will shoot," they say. And he knows they mean it.

He cannot move. He wonders what has happened. Was this the right van? Where is Parks? Has she been arrested too? It doesn't make sense. His back hurts with the weight of the police soldier. His head is pushed into the pavement, his face and eye mashed into the hard concrete surface.

They cuff him. Too tightly. He shrieks out in pain. He looks up to see a machine gun aimed at his face. They haul him off the ground and drag him towards the van. He tries to resist – digging in, helplessly, with his feet, twisting his body down towards the road in one last vain hope. A heavy punch thuds into the back of his head. He loses his sense of the world. All that is left is fear.

How did it come to this?

2.

He sat at his desk in an office 165 floors above the city. He looked out one of the office windows and up at the moon. It was a quarter moon, lying back as if dozing carelessly on the night sky. His eyes darted across the starless heavens to the other moon – the second moon – constructed by a team of astronauts and engineers when he was a young lad. He remembered when they were building it; everyone had been held in collective awe as construction went on, and he had looked up with wonder at the magnificence of mankind, knowing he was a part of history. Then they painted it red and white, with the words *Coca-Cola* emblazoned across the surface.

It was brighter than the old moon yet lacked its authenticity. *They should have spent the money putting an advertisement on the real moon,* he thought. But then maybe that would be too hard – too much paint, too great a distance to travel with all that paint. Plus, he had to admit, the new one was better value: it was perpetually full and round, and the advertisement could be seen nonstop, 24 hours a day – unless it was overcast and covered by clouds, the big cumulonimbus clouds created when rain was required by one of the big corporations. On those days, the whole sky went blank, covering the satellite advertisements like an untouched canvas... beautiful with so much potential. Until it rained, poured where it was needed for crops or industry, then stopped, just as quickly, like a shower tap turned off by an omnipotent God. The God, of course, was the Rain Maker Geoneering Company.

He turned back to his computers. “Log off,” he commanded. He glanced at the clock at the top right of the screen located near his name and employment unit: *Johnson, Information Editing*. It was getting late, and he wanted to get home and relax – watch a show on the HV or muck around on his VR gaming pod. Most of the other employees in his unit had already left for the night. He’d seen them trundle out about an hour earlier, just after 21:00, when the workday ‘officially’ ended.

He walked to the lift, head down, his thoughts filled with the remnants of articles and blogs he’d spent the day editing. He pressed the down button and waited, tapping his feet impatiently on the floor. The lift arrived. The doors opened. There were two other employees in the lift, standing on either side, as if separated by an invisible wall. He didn’t know them, which was understandable, as there were thousands of employees at Gorilla Industries and he barely knew anyone beyond his unit.

He nodded. One nodded back. The other stared straight ahead. *Security,* thought Johnson, and he was hit by a wave of panic.

He wanted to wave them on, get the next lift, but he couldn’t. Not now. It would look suspicious, as if there was something to hide. He got in. The security officer spoke into his earpiece microphone, an index finger pressed down on the other ear. He turned to look straight at Johnson, then the other man. A micro stare on each – just enough to check them both off against the Company data-base.

The lift descended, flowed on for a second, then stopped with a jolt. The doors opened and the security officer alighted, a sneer written across his face. Johnson breathed a sigh of relief and nodded again to his colleague. The colleague stared back.

"Busy day?" Johnson asked, shifting his weight from one foot to the other.

"Always busy here. Too busy," the man replied in a slightly offhand manner. He was stout, like a beer bottle, and balding. Johnson wondered for a second why the man didn't use anti-balding cream or one of the common regrowth tablets.

"They could always hire a few more staff," the man added, pursing his lips.

Johnson was surprised to hear such words from a fellow employee. They were almost treasonous; the sort of thing that could get the man an infraction notice, or worse. Even hearing the words, and not reporting it, was a breach of the employment contract. But there was truth in what the man was saying. They were all working long hours for little reward, with no end in sight. *But what can I do?* Johnson thought. Even if they hired more employees, it wouldn't be more people like them, but robots and automated employee programs – anything to help the Company save on costs.

It took a few minutes for the lift to reach the ground floor. Johnson wanted to ask the bald fellow his name, but felt intimidated or shy, or both. Talking to strangers was not his strong point. And not what you did around the Office Tower. Instead, he blinked on his Eye-Tab. He scrolled over the face-scanner icon set permanently to the main window screen. Thought about opening, then held back. Despite his social awkwardness, this was not how he wanted to learn about his colleagues. But then he blinked, subconsciously, or maybe an accidental twitch of the eye, and before he knew it, the face-scanner had opened. As he looked at the man standing before him, a passport photo appeared in Johnson's vision with various employment details, including the bald man's name, position and unit. He didn't even read the name. He was distracted by a flashing red alert across the bottom of the screen: *TERMINATION WARNING.*

Johnson looked away.

"Did you get a good look at my profile?" asked the man, a psychotic smile wrapped across his hardened face.

"No, no," cried Johnson, his cheeks glowing red. He yearned for the lift to hurry up and reach the ground. It seemed to slow a little in preparation for the final stop, but then took its time to get there, as if the lift was relishing his moment of anguish.

"I'm sorry," Johnson stammered. "It just opened. It was an accident. I never normally use the scanner."

The man shook his head and muttered something under his breath. Something about being no better than the security guard.

The lift finally reached the lobby. Johnson jumped out and bounded across the tiled floor towards the tower exit. The bald man remained, unmoved, as the lift doors shut him out of sight.

Johnson turned off his Eye-Tab with a slow, deliberate blink, in a way thankful now that he hadn't seen the bald fellow's name. It was better this way. He had come across termination warnings before. They were universally dreaded. For those who received them, things usually ended badly: a trail of dissatisfaction following them around, other employees avoiding them as if they had a contagious disease, until, eventually, they were let go and, like a pauper cast out of the city, thrown from their secure homes in the Gorilla Industries Employee Village. He'd heard rumours about the Company raiding their wage accounts to cover any potential losses that might arise from their termination, any overpayments mysteriously realised, and then taking any goods found in their home units, selling the jewellery and expensive items, and sending the rest to the incinerator.

He had seen it all with his friend, Eileen, a few years back. She had been marched out without a chance to collect her things or say goodbye; left with nothing, and probably nowhere to go but the slums. He never found out what happened to her or where she ended up. One moment she was there, a bubbly addition to the Information Team, and the next she was gone: her work email deleted, her social media profiles blocked from the server, her whole existence erased from the Company systems. No one ever spoke of her again. It was as if she never existed, forever deleted from their collective memories ... and from the Gorilla Information Network. But he still remembered her grey bob and little pointy nose, and how she wore a purple felt hat that matched her lipstick. She was like a surrogate mother to him and was one of the few colleagues he'd actually visited in the village. She had told him grand stories of her childhood in Ireland, in the days before the corporations took over everything; when people worked shorter hours and spent whole weekends together, eating and drinking and laughing and singing.

Johnson peered back towards the lift, hoping for another glimpse of the bald man. He was nowhere to be seen. As he reached the door, whispered an apology, and then prayed to the Economy, in hope that the man's warning didn't end up as a full-blown termination. *The chap wasn't particularly nice,* thought Johnson, but he was still a person, and a fellow real-life employee of Gorilla Industries. And no one deserved to live under the constant threat of termination. Johnson felt guilty about the scan, even if it was an accident. It was something he tried to avoid, despite the benefits proliferated by the Company: shopping dollars and bonus points for every face scanned.

Johnson hurried across an open concrete yard that separated the Office Tower and the Employee Village. He breathed out slowly, then sucked in the cool night air. It was only a short walk now to his home unit, and he appreciated the ease with which he could get home. It made the 14-hour days seem a fraction shorter. There was no travel time. No need to catch an electric car or hop on one of the shuttle trains to the outer districts. Especially this late – when the darkness of the night increased the threat of ecoterrorists and anti-globalists, and just being outside the compound walls increased the chances of being caught up in an attack.

He trudged under a boom light that lit up the entire concrete yard. It was empty, save for a few stragglers heading home. Most of his colleagues would already be back in their home units, asleep or watching their holo-visions. There were a couple of others he could see under the yard lights and the radiance of the two moons. They walked towards the village and then turned down little paths or up driveways to their dwellings. Johnson followed. He looked back and recognised Raymond Melville coming from the tower. He was about to stop and wait for him, but Melville was busy on his Eye-Tab. Johnson could see the flashing of light reflected in one of Melville's pupils; could sense the information being fed directly into the eye. He seemed totally absorbed in whatever it was he was watching, like a programmer nutting out code.

Johnson flicked on his own Eye-Tab. A screen appeared in his vision. He could still perceive the world in front of him: the concrete yard, the gate, the neat little houses lined up in rows, the manicured gardens flanked by pink footpaths. But he could also see information superimposed on top; the semitranslucent text and images fanned out across the micro-suburbs of the Employee Village. One reality upon another, both equally his.

"Search news," he said softly, the pin-sized earphone, barely visible in his left ear, picking up the command and sending the orders directly to the Eye-Tab screen. The Gorilla Industries logo sat superimposed at the top left of the digital images appearing on his eye, like a watermark, reminding him of the source. A little gorilla face with fierce black eyes and a bright-yellow banana smile etched into the corner of everything he searched was a small price to pay for nonstop internet access, and an infinite array of information on the glass of his retina. The image flickered in his eye, then transformed into a page with a few news sites listed down the middle. He flicked it to the top corner of the screen with a nonchalant move of the eye, and then waded through the other pages until he reached Rachael's intoxicating face. He blinked her open.

"Today's news, brought to you by Gorilla Industries–" said Rachael.

"Hold on," he said. "I want to watch the Newslink edition, and for you to present it."

"Certainly," she replied. "Would you prefer the full 30-minutes or a shorter version?"

He wondered, for a moment, if she was real: a recording of a voice of a real person, or just another voice created by digital? It made him think of the original Rachael, from high school. They had their first kiss one day after school, on the big green oval where the students played sport. He still remembered the touch of her soft lips on his own; the overwhelming warmth; a moment of infinite beauty held for eternity where they stood, right in the centre of the 'P' in the Paddington Foods sign, which had been permanently embossed onto the synthetic green oval.

He still remembered their lunches too, and the jingle that played on repeat in the school cafeteria: *Lunches, with all a growing kid will need... Paddington Foods, that's Paddington Foods... Lunches, for sustenance and fun. Lunches, with all a growing kid will need...* including his first doses of the dexamphetamine-infused Pep-Me-Up pills that were obligatory in schools to help the children concentrate, and as an aid to the poorly paid teachers before they were unilaterally replaced by the Robotic Teacher System.

His Home Intelligence Unit was now sounding off the various news editions available to him, providing more information in hope of a response. He was barely listening, and instead stared at her face, enamoured by a beauty he'd modelled on the real Rachael from all those years ago. He had re-created her face as best he could through the personalisation settings and endless hours of modification, but she still wasn't quite as he remembered her, no matter what tones and colours he used. He'd flicked between hundreds of shades of brown for her hair and never quite matched it. Her voice was the closest he could find from the pre-set voice settings, but it wasn't quite her ... as if there was some essence to her that couldn't quite be replicated.

"I've actually only got time for the two-minute headlines tonight, Rachael," he said with a craving for any hit of the news - which was the only thing that kept him connected to the world beyond the compound walls.

"The news headlines for Monday, September 5 - brought to you by Denseng, Capital City's own genetic modifier. If you want your children to be the way *you* want them, call Denseng today. They can be as smart, beautiful or successful as you dare to dream–"

"Block ads," he interrupted.

"Ecoterrorists have blown up a Food Inc. production plant, in a follow-up to the Genoma lab-factory attack of 12 days ago. It is believed to be part of an ongoing and coordinated strike on their developments in genetic-based food production.

"In more ecoterrorist-related news, a group of hard-line activists were arrested for their part in an attempt to stifle a mining operation at the Jagulah Lithium Mine. Three protestors were shot on site by Jagulah drones.

"A bomb has gone off in the Banking District. It is believed anti-globalists are behind the explosion. The number of casualties is not yet known. Further details will be available shortly. For ongoing updates on this unfolding crisis, or to purchase anti-blast protection for your home, please click the below link, or say 'anti-globalist' now."

The news was interrupted by a loud beeping sound. For a moment, Johnson thought it was the compound's emergency warning system – but it turned out that the beeping was directly in his ear. It was his in-built Maps system warning him of an approaching gate. "Oh Shit," he said to the air as he looked around, slightly embarrassed by his own lack of awareness.

He scanned his wrist-chip barcode. The gate swung open. "Have a nice evening, Johnson, Information Editor."

The Eye-Tab came back on automatically and Rachael continued: "Google has announced plans for the next phase of its Artificial Intelligence Project, despite the last project being aborted after an off-shelf incident during testing.

"Zhongcom is continuing the development of its own artificial intelligence program in secret. There are concerns this may lead to a further escalation in tensions between ABC Google and Zhongcom – the two technology giants locked in what many are describing as 'the Brain Race'. Chief Executive Hope of the NABOJ Trade Bloc has requested urgent talks between the companies in order to further reduce the risk of an AI-induced singularity.

"In financial news, markets are up again, with the Future Options Exchange receiving a boost after the removal of a temporary bar on double-down futures. Our financial experts have suggested shorting on BMF trades as a result, and to continue selling anything nuclear, due to the ongoing fallout from the Bendowyne Disaster. The sustained global temperature increases have pushed the value of solar energy companies..."

Johnson zoned out. He'd never cared much for the world of finance. It was not like he could get into the share market anyway. He wouldn't have the faintest idea where to begin, even if he did win one of the lotteries he entered each week. Shares were a plaything for the elites and the property owners, not for company serfs like him.

"Can you give me the sports," he blurted out more loudly than necessary.

"In sports," Rachael began, without missing a beat, "the Super International Fight Night Media Frenzy is on tomorrow night, with the fighters coming together from midday for the weigh-ins, and the customary trash talk brought to you by Ham-arm Roids. If you want arms as big as hams, use Ham-arm steroid injections and protein powders."

"And football finals are heating up this weekend, with two elimination matches in the race for the Four Pillars Premiership. On Friday night, the Vitastrength Chargers take on the might of

Amazon-Phizo, while on Saturday the Supplo Giants take on the Bitcoin Golds."

Johnson listened to the rest of the football news, and then ended the broadcast with a double-blink. He rubbed his hands together, excited about watching the big match on Friday night with Conrad, while praying to the Economy for a Chargers victory.

3.

He sees the building up ahead. He checks his tablet screen. The map indicates that he's in the right place. This must be it, he thinks. It's an old hospital. He sees a derelict sign from the days when the Government could afford to run public hospitals, to keep them open for anyone in need. He sees the big sash windows stretched out along each floor of the building, quadrants of glass and wood looked through by a thousand eyes – sick and infirm, and often in times of great pain, but cared for.

In front, between him and the building, is a sandstone wall, grey and covered in moss. He turns back to see his father. He's trotting about 10 yards behind. He looks like he doesn't want to be here. He can feel the energy of despair in the man who raised him, who brought so much fun into his childhood, who danced with joy before...

He doesn't want to think about it, not now, not as he is about to lose his father too. It's not the same, he knows that, but it's still hard to let him go.

"You have to, Dad," he says sadly. "We talked about it. It's the only way."

His father doesn't seem to hear or doesn't want to. His face is glum, his eyes bloodshot. He looks worn out and older than his 76 years; he's aged in the years since she's been gone. His hair is grey and unkempt, and a stubbly white beard has grown haphazardly from the old man's chin. Johnson doesn't remember seeing him shave over the last few months they've stayed together – he'd slept on the couch of the home unit and spent all day watching shows on the holo-vision.

"I am sorry, Dad. You know I want you to stay, but they won't let you. It's the rules. Gorilla Industries won't let anyone stay in the home unit. They did us a favour by letting you stay as long as you did."

His father glances up. A hint of recognition. He knows, he understands. Johnson feels a little relief at this. But he doesn't want to hand him over to the authorities. The Government spends all its money on policing the streets, tracking down terrorists and anti-globalists, and keeping them all 'safe'. Retirement homes are a side issue, not much of a vote winner, as most retirees are barred from the electoral roll. How companies got votes at the expense of people, he'll never know, but that's the way it is these days. And the old folks who matter are in private homes or have company pensions. His dad, and others like him, they don't matter. They are the unwanted, the unneeded, now that they can't work and contribute to economic growth. He just hopes they will treat him well; give him a place to sleep, a comfy bed, shelter, three meals a day, and a holo-vision to watch his shows.

He should never have brought him here, but he can't stop it now. It was the only way. And he tries to explain it: how his father couldn't stay in his solo-home unit, and Johnson couldn't leave his job. He was lucky to get it. The unemployment rate was rising again, and he had only been there a few years. He had to stay put and work his way up. And then maybe he could get a house and move his dad in. He knows that if he had money, they'd bend the rules.

They walk down the driveway together. In silence. The whole place feels eerily silent, reflecting the gravity of it all. Johnson slows, switches the brown suitcase to the other hand. He touches his father gently on the arm. His father walks on, oblivious. They reach the front door. A blackshirt stands there. He holds an automatic rifle across his chest and is wearing infra-red goggles, a helmet and a thick grey vest. Johnson can just about make out his face. He thinks of his brother in the Home Security Office, wishes he was here, so they could take their father in together... knowing then that he would be treated well.

They walk down a long green corridor. The paint is faded. It stills smells of disinfectant. He senses the day when it was a thriving hospital. Empty now. It is a cold and lifeless corridor with doors leading to nowhere. They reach the end and turn left. A sign directs them – Retiree Check-In. They blunder through a double door. His father drops behind again. He doesn't want to go. Johnson can sense his father's anxiety. Why would he want to go? There will be nothing there but misery and boredom. He can imagine a small room with a bed and a chair and a kitchenette, some old blankets, an HV... no... an old television in the corner. But what can be done? He has no choice.

"Come on, Dad," he says.

His father picks up the pace a little, stays with him.

They follow the signs left, then right, then up some metal stairs. They arrive at a door with another blackshirt. Johnson looks up at the guard and searches in vain for eyes, which remain hidden. The blackshirt is motionless, an empty vessel.

Johnson opens the door and they walk in. A room opens up before them. It is wide, with seats, like a waiting room. A receptionist is sitting behind a clear plastic desk. There are two groups of people waiting in makeshift lines separated by bollards. A security guard stands at the back of the room, beside a body scanner and conveyer belt.

Johnson places the bag, his father's last belongings, on the ground next to him, and they line up in groups – a cacophony of old people scattered with family members who have shown up for the handover. It is like an airport. The air is filled with the hollowness of departure.

They wait while the people in front check in their parents. He sees them signing paperwork, sheet after sheet, signed and co-signed by all those present, and then one by one they are led away. There are tears and hugs. He knows he should be talking to his father, telling him how much he loves him, but he can't. He doesn't know what to say. Their last minutes together are ticking by, and they wait in silence...

4.

Johnson looked at his face in the mirror. It was pasty, almost colourless. He didn't get enough sun, even with the sun-replacement tablets he took. He considered the natural, unfiltered reflection before him. His close-cut hair suited his well-shaped head. He rubbed his hands over it, felt the prickles of short hair against his fingers. His face was angular, ragged almost, but he still looked younger than his years. His light facial hair was too thin to form a proper beard. He knew he wasn't ugly, but he wasn't handsome either. He had seen handsome in the fashion magazines. It was dark-haired and dark-skinned with an arched nose, or tall and blond with a powerful square jaw... none of which he had.

He thought about last night dream with his father. Why he chose to dream about his father on the Dream Weaver, he'd never know. It was always the sad memories that came – never the happy ones. Next time, he'd just stick to dreaming about Rachael – artificial dreams too, not even based on reality. Ones where they stayed together, and he was living a different life. With her. Far away from his current reality.

"Turn on holo-vision," he commanded as he headed back to the main room. An entire wall of his house lit up like a computer screen, the content projected outwards in three-dimensional beauty. The Gorilla Industries logo appeared as a background to the various icons scattered throughout. They were arranged haphazardly, in contrast to the order of the rest of the house. He glanced at the gambling porthole, at the far right of the giant screen, where he could play online poker or make bets on live sports matches. Below it and out a little further was an icon of a ripe orange mango that loaded Mango Search. His eyes moved along to the 3DBR-HV-link and the promise of endless shows and movies told in staggering beyond-world beauty. There was so much to watch, more than was possible if he lived a dozen long lifetimes and spent every second glued into the screen.

He called for Rachael and watched as her beautiful, digital face materialised in front of him.

"How can I help?"

He felt a surge of joy at her presence. She might only be an In-Tech Intelligent Design Home Control & Information Unit, and not even the latest model, but she was his. She was always with him – in his eye, in his ear, almost in his brain. She kept him company and was online when he demanded, connecting him to a world he barely saw beyond the compound walls, and answering his questions, whatever they may be. She made him smarter too. He knew what she knew, which was pretty much everything readable, downloadable or searchable on the internet.

"Two pieces of brown rye toast please, Rachael."

Better have a banana as well, he thought, remembering an online health forum that recommended at least one piece of fruit each morning. He peeled the banana slowly, admiring the perfect smile as the skin fell away. The bioengineers at Gorilla Industries had released the 'smile-nanas' in response to The Apple's oversized novelty apples that came in a hundred different colours and flavours – a marketing gimmick that meant he was never short of the yellow fruit.

4.

He heard a rumble and looked up to see the bread drop from the self-serving fridge into the automatic toaster. He sat, eating his banana, waiting for the bread to toast. A few minutes later, Rachael told him it was ready.

"There is only one piece of bread left. Shall I order some more?" she asked.

"That would be good," he answered. He lathered the toast with margarine, imagining the day that one of the big appliance companies would develop a toaster that could actually spread on the topping. He could see it now – a robotic toaster with little arms on each side. He laughed. *It couldn't be too far off,* he thought. *After all, they'd sent someone to Mars.*

"What is making you laugh?" Rachael asked.

"Oh nothing, really. Can you make it a loaf of double-yeast bread, oil-infused? And how much are avocados? Still too expensive, right?"

"They have not dropped to your usual price limit. They are well over 75 International Dollars each at every outlet within a 50-kilometre radius, and nearly all are saying they are sold out."

"When do they expect supply to increase?" he asked, munching on his toast.

"Avocado production remains down since one of Genoma's local food production factories was blown up by ecoterrorists on the 24th of August–"

Johnson had heard about it on the news nearly every day since the attack – saturation coverage, as was the case with all ecoterrorist and anti-globalist activity.

"Why did they do it?" he asked, as much to himself.

Rachael explained that New Dawn – the ecoterrorist group that had claimed responsibility for the attack – was angry about food being made by scientists in test tubes rather than grown by farmers on the land.

"What about natural avocados?" Johnson asked.

"Most natural plantations in the Food Bowl were destroyed in the summer by a series of ultra-cyclones."

Johnson sighed. Despite the frightening tales he heard daily about the ecoterrorists, a part of him wondered if they were the last ones left fighting for something worthwhile. He'd supported them, years ago, when the last wild animals were near extinction, and they were still called ecowarriors. That was a cause that regular people could get behind. No one wanted to see a world without giraffes and hippopotamuses – even if they were mostly seen on the Nature Channel through the eyes of a reanimated and permanently aged David Attenborough. But this cause had fallen away after the scientists managed to replicate those endangered species – creating new ones from DNA, inserting them into surrogates, and then refilling the zoos and the last few nature reserves. And the ecoterrorists had turned their attention to the geneticists and food scientists who, they said, were "playing God". Johnson remembered seeing holo-vision coverage of their early protests – before laws banning them under threat of arrest were enacted – where long-haired dissenters with colourful, patchy clothes held up signs: *The Earth is a Garden NOT a Lab,* and *First Food, Then People.*

"Anything else you want me to order?" Rachael asked. Her voice coming to him from the surround-sound speakers he'd installed to give her voice greater depth, make him feel less alone in his home unit night after night. Sadly, he couldn't see that changing. His only date in the past year had been an absolute disaster, and despite many hours of flicking through profiles on his online dating app, hesitating with his finger hovered over the faces of a dozen different girls, he couldn't bring himself to take the plunge and ask any of them for an online face-chat.

He sauntered over to the pantry and looked inside. It was almost bare, apart from the beers that filled up one shelf, a few long-date tomatoes that he hadn't got around to eating, and never seemed to go off, and a host of unused condiments. "You'd better order a mixed 10-pack of Finer Diner dehydrated meals for one, four solo pre-cooked pastas, six sachets of single-serve pre-cooked rice, four sing-tins of Tiny Tuna, two small cans of baked beans, my usual frozen pizza, one medium beefo pie, a glacial melt... a box of Twisters, and I was thinking of getting a mineral booster as well."

"Any particular brand?"

"Vitastrength, of course," he said, "to support the Chargers," he added with a grin.

"They have multiple options. The most popular is the ZMI Mineral Supplement, which has an overall rating of 4.73 stars across both Mango Rate and Google Shout."

"That will do."

"The order has been placed and will be delivered on the next available drone."

He could hear the drones outside. Even this early in the morning they were out – thousands of them crisscrossing the sky, like bees in a meadow before the mass extinction, delivering breakfast or make-up, or shoes, or batteries, or beer or Pep-Me-Up pills... whatever a consumer wanted. He could also hear the Company security 'wasp' drones, and the police 'hornets', which kept an eye out for breaches of the peace, their rotating facial recognition cameras on constant alert, with sleep darts and bullet-missiles at the ready. They were lower in tone. Cold, grey metal machines, inhuman, emotionless robots designed to watch and hunt and even kill. They scared him; reminded him of a horrible accident he'd witnessed years ago, when an out-of-control drone, the size of a car, had crashed into an old man on the pavement in front of him. The old man had been smashed to smithereens, cut apart by the rotating blades as if he were a giant lab-egg being whisked up to make an omelette.

Johnson showered quickly, put on his navy pants, pleather belt, and grey shirt with the Gorilla Industries logo. He shivered in the morning cool and pulled on a thin woollen knit jumper. It had a small hole under the arm and was probably ready for the bin. *If only I could sew,* he thought, as he pinched at the hole, remembering all the sewing his mother had done before she died. She had gone into a fit – knitting scarves and jumpers and sewing together quilts from old bits of fabric she kept in the 'scrap box'. She had said she wanted to create something for the grandchildren to remember her by, and she had looked accusingly at Johnson, as if being single was his choice.

Johnson fumbled around with his shoes.

"Would you like the news headlines this morning?" Rachael asked.

Johnson stood up quickly. "I need to get to work. And it's always the same news anyway. Probably another ecoterrorist attack," he said with a droll chuckle.

"The daily news is different each day, and there have been no confirmed reports of any ecoterrorist attacks since Thursday's attack on the Food Inc. production plant," Rachael replied, missing his sarcasm.

"Okay, right. Bye," said Johnson as he walked over to the front door, preparing himself for another long day of work. He noticed the time on his Eye-Tab. It was 06:53 – he had to get going if he wanted to avoid a late fine.

"Shall I order dinner for your arrival tonight, then?" she asked.

"No, I've got to go," he snapped.

"My voice analysis is detecting high stress levels, Johnson. Would you like me to order something for this?"

"No, I'll be okay," he said. "Sorry," he added. He didn't need to apologise – it was not as if his Home Intelligence Unit could get offended, but he still liked to treat her well and felt guilty when he didn't. The online training video had said it was best to behave as if they were a friend, for this would provide the best end-user experience. It even suggested he design her to look and sound like a real person, preferably someone he knew – which he had done – for this would help them adapt more naturally to human emotions.

He'd often thought about getting her animated into a silicone body so he could sit next to her on the couch when they conversed, or they could lie in bed and cuddle up when he needed companionship or sex. But he didn't have the money. And a part of him knew that if he had her like that – in body form – it would be as if he were giving up on the chance of true love and the possibility, no matter how remote, of finding someone as mesmerising as the real Rachael had been all those years ago.

5.

Una pulled back the blind, making sure there were no drones, and looked out the window. Her eyes traversed the huge mounds of fallow earth on the horizon; the monotonous brown punctuated by the odd tuft of yellow grass. The land had been dug up and bulldozed into unnatural, godless shapes, which were now weathering like old men slowly crumpling to the ground.

In the distance was Lake Santos – or 'the lake', as she called it. There was a beauty in its shimmering water, at least from where she stood – where the early-morning sunlight sparkled on its surface – but the closer you got, the uglier it became. The water was undrinkable too, a large well with a horrid grey chemical sludge lying beneath. She swam in it once, when she first arrived, and felt the grey chemical sludge on her feet. She wanted to feel free after escaping the city. But it was risky and stupid, and she spent the rest of the day in the bath, scrubbing her body, hoping not to get sick.

She breathed in gently. There was an acrid smell that stuck like sandpaper in the nostrils. "You get used to the smell," she would tell new arrivals, always reminding them that the smell had its purpose too, keeping the place hidden from prying eyes and unwanted visitors. And then she told them the all-important ground rules: Always be vigilant. Keep away from the windows. Watch for hornets and wasps… even delivery drones and bees should be avoided. Limit outside movement. Paint the walls regularly with the metallic camouflaging paint that kept them and their equipment safe from automated spies. And finally, no personal information, no real names.

She looked at the barren landscape, imagining its heyday before the bulldozers and diggers came in, before they extracted every mineral and sucked out every last drop of life.

She heard a creaking sound behind her. She let go of the blind and turned to see a man standing in the doorway. He was dark-featured, with heavy jowls and lips, and thick black hair pushed back. He nodded. "What are you up to?"

"Just enjoying the unspoilt air," she answered with a wry smile.

He made a sound - a *harrumph* of sorts - his eyes not meeting hers. He stood there for a few moments, looking at the floorboards, one hand latched onto the architrave by his side.

"You're Camus, right?"

He nodded. "Can we have some help with the filming?"

"Sure. What do you need?"

"We need some more light... basically, if you can hold the light stand that will help."

Una nodded, left behind her sanctuary at the window - complete with 365-degree views of the mined-out deserts of hell, like Mordor - and floated across the bare, mostly wooden room. She followed Camus out the door and down the long hallway, along an old carpet stained with red wine.

"Is Parks doing the vision-stream?" she asked.

"No. She's in the city - on a mission."

"Which mission?"

"The retirement homes."

"Is she in a safe house?" Una asked nervously.

"Parks, I believe, is with her grandmother. Preparing for the handover.

Una sighed. She knew what Parks was doing was dangerous. And it must have been traumatic for her too – and dreadful for her grandma. They were brave souls. But she knew her friend would be happy to die for the cause. They all would be. There were some things more important than living. What was one life compared with the soul of humanity, and their collective futures? This was the humanist way. "The greater good," she said, repeating their mantra aloud.

"Amen to that," Camus replied as they reached the big open-living space that doubled as their studio. She sat down on one of the blue couches.

Camus went over to the filming equipment. "Here, hold this," he said as he passed her a large backlight.

She grabbed it with both hands. "Who's filming it?"

"Lenmar!"

"Wow!"

"Yep, the Renegade himself," said a strong voice from behind them. It was Lenmar, strutting across the room in his red bandit mask – the mask that turned him into the Renegade. He didn't need it – he could always get a new face – but it had become part of who he was, part of the mythology.

Una turned around and gave him a hug. "What's the stream about today?"

"The usual," he said with a grin. "Why the system is fucked. And why we've got to break it down... one greedy, profit-seeking company at a time." His grin turned fierce, and his eyes burnt with fire. It was one reason he was able to inspire so many. There was passion and belief in all he did, and that passion burst forth from his eyes, from his essence, across computers and LAN/S-pods and holo-visions and wall screens, and into the hearts of those who saw their films – the truth, as they called it, or the word, the real word and not the 'Economist' garbage sprouted forth by the neo-liberalists that ran the world.

"For the greater good," she said, bowing her head slightly in deference to Lenmar.

"For the greater good," he replied. He stood zen-like before them. It wasn't long before the room was crammed with other humanists eager to see the Renegade in action.

"Where's my beret, and the flag?" The Renegade said. There was a flurry of action and then someone ran forward and handed them to him. "You ready, Camus?" he said, as he put the beret with the black and white boot-print on his head.

"Ready. Can you stand over there? And I need you here," Camus said as he pointed Una across the room. "And try not to move."

"Why would I move–" she began testily, before Lenmar cut her off, his hands outstretched towards them. "My friends, it's time to band together," he said, looking at them both, then, turning sharply to the camera, "and rise up!"

6.

He flicked on two computer screens – one directly in front of his face and one on the desk beneath his hands. He placed his thumbs on the print pads, and then watched as his face was scanned by the screen. "Live DNA scan required." He placed his finger in the small hole, felt a slight pinch, and then waited while they matched his DNA against the system. 'Welcome Johnson – Information Editor' appeared on the screen, then disappeared, replaced with the icons and windows he would be using throughout the day. An email popped up. It was a list of tasks from his boss, the Information Manager, whom he had never met, and might not even be human – just some binary code linked to an email.

He began looking through each news item presented to him by the online database, reading carefully, examining the general content, making sure it was suitable for the Gorilla Information Network, discarding any material that was unsavoury or not in keeping with the Company's ideals. Of course, he had to check over any specific mentions of Gorilla Industries or its competitors – The Great Library and the other regulated internet channels – and the key buzzwords for the industry. But he also had to track any new websites and blogs, even comments or social posts, being uploaded along the entire Information Network, reporting or exhuming anything that could be deemed 'dangerous to social or economic harmony'.

6.

His job was easier now that a computer program scanned through the millions of online documents uploaded each day and flagged any 'risky' stories. When he first started at Gorilla Industries, he had to read through all the material being loaded to the network himself. Back then, the Information Editing Team had been huge, but there were mass redundancies following the introduction of the scanning software, and now there were only a few employees left. The researchers and information scanners had been the first to go, then the older employees and those close to gaining their Company pensions. It had put a grey cloud of despondency over the entire unit, but no one said anything. They all knew that it was better to keep quiet and keep your job, to avoid ending up out in the slums or living on the streets. There were nasty rumours about what they did to those on the streets, unable to afford shelter, with no protection or refuge – rumours that filled him with dread; of vagrants disappearing and being used for genetic testing by Genoma or Denseng or, worst of all, by companies dabbling in hybrid artificial intelligence, where he could be spliced up with an animal – half rat, half human – or his brain might end up in a machine, living forever in a permanent state of desolation until the sun exploded.

Fortunately, for now, they still needed Johnson, and the others in his unit, to look after the remaining edits and to create new content for the sites, including branded material for the companies paying big bucks to promote their products on the network. It kept him employed and sheltered, although the threat of job automations was ever present, in the same way that car-driving had been automated when he was a boy.

The first thing he read was a social media post about a gorilla that had escaped Ledtown Zoo and was on the loose – which should never have reached him. He read some background direct from the zoo. It was one of the last naturally born gorillas on the entire continent, and the zoo was desperate to keep its star attraction alive. They had requested that civilians keep watch, company drones keep away, and police security drones use sleep darts rather than the bullet-missiles they preferred. *Someone will have to pay a lot for that sort of disruption of the peace*, thought Johnson, as he waved it through onto the Gorilla Information Network.

He clicked through to the next story that appeared in his feed. It was from an autonomous news site called *The Untouched Gazette;* an opinion piece about the problems with the major information servers and the sanctioned media. One paragraph, which required significant editing, read:

Information providers, like Gorilla Industries and The Great Library, have failed the needs of the masses. They have destroyed the last vestiges of the free and unregulated internet, claiming at first that they would provide a platform for all. However, they are not providers of information, as may be implied by the name, but vassals for the corporations and the elites that run most of these companies. So invested are they in putting out good stories that support their own assets, that they will now only provide access to certain information in keeping with their ideals. They delete or remove anything of concern, expunging any memory of the offending material, such that it is forever banished to the ether. Other companies have caught on to this way and now pay the big information providers to do the same for them. It makes you wonder, when watching the news, if you are really watching the news, or just fake-news, and whether there is any real information being provided at all, or just a smoking pile of misinformation.

6.

He logged in to the website through a server 'back door' and removed any reference to Gorilla Industries in the story. He read through it again, removing the worst paragraphs and editing out the overt disdain for information providers as he went. He could delete the whole thing, but he preferred to be subtle and not entirely destructive to a writer's creation.

The coffee-bot drove past his desk. He waved it over and had it fill his mug – with the original blue Capital City Chargers football team logo on it. *Extra-strong, double shot, black, without any of that awful cow-less, dairy-free, genetically modified milk* – the bot knew his order. It was the same, twice daily.

He drank his coffee in spurts between edits and approvals, moving on quickly when editing was not required, interrupted only by the blaring of the intercom: "Gorilla Industries would like to thank this week's employee of the month, Fox from Provider Support, who scanned a record number of faces for the internal recognition system, and will receive a $500 Gorilla bonus for his efforts. Well done, Fox!"

Johnson popped a tranquilium anti-anxiety tablet from his medicine drawer. He didn't like to take them at work, but he was fretting over the next round of announcements.

A few minutes later, as if on cue, the intercom boomed out across the office floor: "Gorilla announcement, Gorilla announcement. Attention all staff. The following employees will be terminated with immediate effect..."

Johnson rubbed anxiously at his forehead, wondering what names would be on that list – and whether the bald man would be one of them. He remembered the day when his friend, Eileen, had been on that list; when he'd been forced to watch on, helplessly, as she was dragged away from her desk by the Company Soldiers.

It was in the afternoon, after he'd popped his second Pep-Me-Up pill, when Johnson found the footage. It was uploaded to him for approval or editing as normal, but it caught his attention immediately. It was a live stream and had been posted on an unknown site by 'the Renegade'. The Renegade wore a mask, like a bandit, and a beret, and ranted about the state of the world. But Johnson could see his eyes. They gleamed with furious passion.

He spoke violently at the screen: "The big companies are colluding to keep wages down. Some even paying their employees in food and lodging and nothing more. Employees locked in compounds, working 90 hours a week, with only one day off at the end. And they say this isn't slavery, that every employee chooses to work in these appalling conditions.

"Well, that's rubbish. Slavery is back, and the corporate oligarchy and the elites that are running these companies are enslaving an entire generation of workers to keep themselves rich. This world is more unequal than at any time in history. Only feudal times compare. And we all know what happened to the Tsar."

Johnson thought of his own life lived between the Office Tower and the employee compound, and then turned his mind back to the audio-visual recording.

"The Government legislated against this sort of exploitation, but now this same Government has been corrupted. The politicians are owned by wealthy landowners and the corporate elite – lobbied and paid directly to act in their interests. The Government isn't going to stop them. Who do you think pays the politicians, keeps them in fancy houses and cars, pays for their holidays and security guards? Who gives them their dodgy elections? Who reads out the results of elections that never happened? The same corporations benefiting from a rigged system are the ones that have been granted unparalleled access and even voting rights... this was meant to be a democracy of the people, not of business, for the many, not the few. We, the people, don't seem to matter any longer."

The man in the mask held up a small banner. It was the anti-globalist underground banner with a black boot print on a red-and-white striped background. It was an image Johnson knew, one they had all been taught to fear – one associated with explosions and the deaths of the innocent.

He went on: "These mega-conglomerates and financial institutions give the Government enough money to plaster our walls with nonsense slogans and saturate the internet and information providers with made-up news stories. They blame us for their failings. Who benefits from the system? Not you, not me, but the companies and property tycoons that control this world."

The man in the mask went quiet, then stared down the screen and spoke in a voice quivering with emotion: "You want change, then you have to make that change, my friends and equals. Rise up and join the fight against the global corporatocracy. Bring down the elites! Rise up! Spread the word."

Johnson immediately flagged the footage and sent it to his manager marked dangerous. It was the sort of content that would go all the way to the top of Gorilla Industries, and then end up in the hands of the police or the Anti-Terror Squad. And if it was deemed a legitimate threat, then it would end very badly for the masked reactionary. Johnson knew there was truth in what this 'renegade' said, but there was not much he could do about it. It was part of his job to filter out 'dangerous material'. They were 'economic terrorists', as Sky-Fox Media had dubbed them, or anti-globalists, as most people called them – dissidents and agitators trying to bring down the global capitalist system. Johnson didn't agree with everything, especially the long hours of work for little reward, and the entrenched inequality, with vast sums of wealth being amassed by the elites while many struggled to get by. But without the free market and the deregulated global economy, they might all be in slums. "The rising tide lifts the boats," is what they said in the School of Economics sermons when they talked about the way wealth trickled down from the top.

He felt guilty now, as it dawned on him that he may be condemning this unknown stranger to an awful fate. But he had to pass it up the chain. It was his job. If he didn't, he would face the wrath of his employer or, worse, a visit from the black-shirted soldiers of the Home Security Office. But even so, a little part of him wanted to see it one more time. There was something intriguing about the Renegade in his red cloth mask and beret; those gleaming eyes, piercing the screen between them; his powerful voice filled with rage as he called for people to rise up. There was an undying power in his essence; it gave Johnson a strange feeling, a sense of which he couldn't quite grasp... a feeling he hadn't felt for a long time.

He clicked the play button again. Nothing! It had been blocked. He hit his hands down on the desk in frustration, slightly louder than he intended. "Aggaarp," he cursed quietly under his breath, turning suddenly to make sure no one had heard him. The room was quiet, as always, but no faces turned his way; they were all locked into their own computers, unaware of anything beyond their screens.

7.

Your artificial intelligence robot is not just a lover, but also a friend and companion. With statistics showing that those with an in-home AI lover are 70% happier than those in relationships...

Johnson continued to edit the document, thinking, for a moment, how nice it would be if he could get Rachael converted into his own personal robot-lover.

He rubbed his eyes. He was struggling to read the font and wondered if he should get his eyes refocused. Maybe he was just tired. "Enlarge the screen size by 50%," he commanded his PC unit. The text of the news article suddenly ballooned out before his eyes. He stepped back automatically. It was a little too big. He couldn't see half the article he was editing – it drifted into the ether beyond the sides of his main screen, with the bottom third falling onto the desk screen below. "Adjust screen," he said, and the open page bounced back to full-screen mode.

He looked over the supportive material forwarded to him by the Research and Development Team, trying to find a pie chart or graphic to support the statistics. He really needed a short romantic video from the Video Editing Team. The more videos and graphics, the more likely it would get traction on the Gorilla Information Network.

He still had to do a paid piece for Sunshine Retirement Homes but kept putting it off. The paid content was another way Gorilla Industries made money, using its network channels and influence on the Regulated Internet, the RegNET as they called it, to push news stories, change and create information, and of course, advertise – or "Always Be Advertising", as the Information Manager stated in any emails regarding new content. Johnson didn't mind – content creation was always juicier, although most of that work had now been automated too. And his role was confined more and more to editing and moderating. Which of course he was good at: a combination of creative and written skills and the right personality – whatever that meant – as diagnosed when he first joined the Gorilla Industries family. He'd been through two interviews, a security scan, Home Security clearance, an online personality test and a six-hour-long digital exam. Then they'd sent him up to the 165th floor and the Information Editing Unit, and it had been his office home nearly every day since.

His head nodded forward; his concentration was waning again. He opened his desk drawer and took out the vial of Pep-Me-Up pills. He looked the bottle over and then placed it back down by his desk. *Do I really need one?* he wondered. A part of him didn't want to take it, nor any of the pills they gave him, but they had their benefits too – they helped him stay on task and get through the day, kept his mood up. It was a hard choice.

He stood up and stretched his back. *Maybe I should go for a walk,* he thought, trying to find a distraction. The Company had a way of making you feel you were trespassing when you went anywhere but 'your designated work zones'. But today he needed it. And he could just go outside for a moment, get some fresh air; and have a quick scoot around the courtyard between the tower and the Employee Village; enjoy the isolation while everyone was still on the job, before the hurried action at the end of the workday, when it filled with worker ants trudging back to their home units and families and holo-visions – whatever kept them company in those few hours of freedom before bed.

Johnson turned around to check if anyone was looking, and then slinked towards the office door, hoping no one would see him. There were no specific rules against him leaving his desk, but it still felt wrong: 'An employee was privileged to have a job and that privilege could be taken away at any time.'

It's just a short break to get my editing mojo back, he told himself as he headed down in the lift.

He reached the courtyard. The sun was setting behind the Employee Village. The golden ball of radiant energy sank into a line of uniform geoneered clouds. Pink rays spun out in all directions, covering the bottom of the sky – behind and beneath the Coca-Cola moon the other satellite advertisements – with coral and salmon and daubs of purple, before the indigo of the coming night took hold and flowed across the remaining heavens. *It's beautiful,* he thought. He so rarely got to see a sunset; he had forgotten the majesty of colour and the sublime beauty of the whole experience – even if much of the magic was caused by the city's main rain supplier.

He walked by the tennis court and pool complex that was reserved for senior management, then turned along the edge of the open courtyard. He peered out at the array of houses and gardens and the neat paths that linked them together like a miniature settlement. He couldn't quite see his solo-unit house from here, but it wasn't far.

As he thought about returning to the office, a woman in a suit and dark glasses marched towards him. It was Security.

She looked at him. Her face was stern. "Step aside, sir," she said firmly.

There was a commotion behind. He looked past the security guard to see a man being dragged by two Company soldiers dressed in their yellow-and-brown fatigues. The man was stocky and bald, and appeared to be resisting the soldiers. One of the soldiers put his arm under the man's chin, and blasted him with a quick shot of pain from his electrified wrist guard. The man slumped forward, his head lolling from side to side as if he were an unused puppet. The only hint of life was a steady stream of drool coming from the man's mouth.

Johnson didn't want to look at the soldiers, but as they passed by, he glanced up and recognised the man being dragged away. It was the bald man from the lift. He cast his eyes down to the concrete.

A scream echoed around the courtyard. Johnson looked up again. The bald man was staring, his eyes hollow, pleading for help with every last gasp of strength. Johnson thought he caught a hint of recognition in the man's eyes. There was nothing he could do for him. He slowed and shook his head, as if trying to convey the impossibility of the situation, the powerlessness of them both. *What was his name?* Johnson tried desperately to remember. But he didn't know. He never had. He felt a gut-wrenching pain in his stomach – for his own failures, for not being able to do anything, for not even really knowing who he was.

"Help me!" shouted the bald fellow.

Johnson tightened up, and then watched helplessly on as one of the soldiers smashed the man's jaw. He heard it crunch into a dozen pieces, and the man go silent.

The other soldier turned towards Johnson. "What are you doing?" he bellowed. "You want a dose of this?" He held up his arm, showing the electrified wrist guard, and the pain he had the power to administer.

“No, no. I’m just going back to work,” Johnson stammered.

As he rushed towards the office building, he heard the man pleading for his things. His voice was slightly muffled now, as if it were a strain to speak. His plight was grim. Johnson knew it and the man knew it too. Google knows what they would do with him before they tossed him out onto the street.

8.

Johnson lay in bed, his mind wasted from too many tranquilium pills washed down with beer after beer in a futile attempt to drown his thoughts – thoughts about the bald man being dragged away by the Company soldiers. He didn't want to think about it, or anything.

He'd even been thinking about the Renegade clip – and ways he could see it again outside the network. He was a little surprised by this – as if he wasn't thinking straight or maybe there was something exciting in the Renegade himself that was forcing him down an unexpected and potentially dangerous tangent. Of course, he knew the stream had already been blocked from the Gorilla Information Network, a soon as he had passed it up the chain at work. There was no way he could see it again unless Rachael could find it on another network or out in the dark web – and he'd even thought of asking her this. But he couldn't risk searching it from his home unit. It was far too risky. They monitored everything. And he couldn't access other networks or information providers from his home network. But then he wondered if he could use the old unused internet tablet that his Dad had given him, before he'd gone into the home, connect it up to the RegNET from an outside web source, and see if there were any more of the Renegade's films out there.

He eventually pushed these insidious thoughts away and turned again to the Dream Weaver. His only solace in sleep.

8.

But this time, he wanted a happy memory, of family, of a better time. He clicked on the remote, put the headset over his head, and then lay back, waiting for sleep to arrive and take him to the land of dreams...

He is standing in the backyard of his family home. His brother, Goliath, kicks a ball to him across the well-kept grass, and then barges over, following the ball. Johnson tries to dart past his older brother, but trips over, and then Goliath falls on top of him and they wrestle, both laughing in a mess of blue – as always, they are both wearing their Capital City Chargers jerseys.

His father is on the deck, admiring the moment. He comes over and grabs the ball away from them, and then runs off with it, following a long, playful arc around the yard. "I've got it now, boys," he says, and they chase him together. His father slows and the two of them pounce, but his dad's smile stretches on forever, as if there is no place else he'd rather be. It makes Johnson smile too – he loves Sundays with all the family playing around together in the backyard, with everyone home and the house filled with a hive of noise and activity.

"Have you laid the table yet?" his mum yells from the kitchen.

His dad pauses, takes a deep breath. "Okay boys, we'd better lay the table."

Goliath tries to grab the ball one more time. His dad just laughs and gives it to him. "Come on, we can play after lunch." He grabs Goliath and gives him a bear hug, and Johnson feels left out, but his dad notices and pulls him in as well.

Goliath breaks away and they walk over to the raised deck area. Johnson helps his dad set the table. He puts the plates out around the recently oiled square wooden table – five seats today because Nana is here too. His father walks behind him, meticulous and brisk in the way he puts the cutlery out. Then he darts inside to get the glasses and lemon water. And Johnson follows, eager to help his father, eager to please – the good son. The same can't always be said for his brother, but Goliath is being friendly today and that is enough, especially recently, when he seems to have finally outgrown his younger brother... or at least prefers his bedroom and a closed door to chatting about football and their movie heroes.

His mum comes out with a dish of steaming vegetables. She places it on a round cork mat in the middle of the table. She stands, her hands on hips, perusing the table with a beaming, round, love-filled face. "We need another mat," she says matter-of-factly. Then, seeing only one son helping, she adds: "Can you get me a mat, Goliath."

"Where do I get it?" Goliath replies.

"Third drawer in the kitchen, by the oven," she replies. "Come, I need to get the rest of the food."

And Goliath follows his mother back through the screen door. He will always be his mother's son. They even look alike – the same auburn hair and freckly skin – while Johnson is more like his father.

A moment later, mother and son return with the pièce de résistance: creamy fish stew – one of his mum's classic meals – and hot bread with real butter. Johnson licks his lips in anticipation and looks up at the beautiful blue sky – which stretches untouched from one horizon to the other. Almost too perfect.

9.

The Chargers' forward intercepted the ball and zoomed up the sideline, dodging defenders as he went. He darted inside towards the goal, but just as he was about to shoot, an Amazon-Phizo defender swooped in at an almighty speed and knocked him over.

"Penalty!" yelled Johnson as the robo ref whistled for half-time.

"See where that guy came from to make that tackle... he was juiced up on speed enhancers for sure," Conrad said from his position on the green AppChat window that cut into one side of the wall screen; a toothy grin and blond mop top looking down at Johnson like a gargoyle.

"How do we compete with that?" said Johnson. "Their players are all doped up to their eyeballs on the latest Phizo Pharmaceuticals gear."

"Vitastrength needs to put our players on the same stuff," Conrad replied.

"Yeah, true, but we also want to win fair," Johnson added.

"Ha! Good luck with that," said Conrad. "But there's always hope. It's only half-time, and there's always our boy, ZMI Domingo."

Johnson nodded.

"Should we have a bet?" Conrad asked. The football pitch was immediately replaced by a colourful sponsored link to Super Bet, and a voice yelling the latest in-play match odds.

"Nah, I can't face betting against the Chargers," said Johnson.

"I'll have a bet on the final score... and I think I'll throw some on the Armadillos. Then, either way, it's a win," boomed Conrad with the confidence Johnson so admired. They had seen so much together over the years, particularly in their younger days, before life became work, when they spent their entire school holidays kicking a football or playing computer console games. Mostly they had played *LAM Sports Football*, arguing over who would get to play as the Capital City Chargers, before agreeing to play in partnership, as a team, against whatever the computer could throw at them, fighting desperately for a shot at the Four Pillars Premiership – something that had always eluded the real Chargers.

Conrad placed his bets, while Johnson's attention was blasted by an advertisement for The Big Fridge Company's latest self-cooking kitchens. Johnson's thoughts immediately turned to his now pressing need for the Ramsay-Master Smarter Kitchen, and whether his credit cards could take such a purchase.

Fortunately, Conrad caught his attention again from the big screen. "How are things at Chimp Industries?" he asked.

"Gorilla Industries," replied Johnson sternly, "and you'd better be careful saying things like that. This is a Gorilla screen I'm talking to you on..."

"I know, I know, I was just joking. Where's your sense of humour gone, Jay?"

"Sorry. I am just being careful at the moment. I saw a fellow terminated the other day. It was brutal. It shook me up a bit. Got to be careful, that's all. I can't risk losing my job, you know. It's all I've got." He sat up and scratched his head.

"Don't worry, Jay. They need you to keep the internet free

of rubbish."

"Ha! Thanks, Conrad. Anyway, forget that. It's going to be a good night. We've still got another half of football to watch."

"Go Chargers!" Conrad yelled.

Johnson whooped. "How's The Marketplace?" he asked. "You still selling everything in the world?"

"Of course! 'Whatever you need, we've got it,'" Conrad replied.

"Avocados?" Johnson asked with a grin.

"Yeah, I wish. Don't get me started. I could have as many of them as I wanted if it wasn't for those damn ecoterrorists blowing shit up. You know what I'd like to do with them... round them all up and well–"

Johnson jumped in, mumbling something about the mega cyclones contributing to the loss of crops, sounding as Rachael would in this moment.

"The ecoterrorists did their part, as they always do. And what's wrong with you today, Johnson. You sound like an apologist for them."

Johnson's face reddened. "Not me. I've just got to keep you on track, Conrad," he said with a giggle. "Otherwise, who knows what I am going to hear."

"That's why you enjoy my company," said Conrad between mouthfuls of chips.

"I do. And what about all those employees in your team on the factory floor. Do they still like your company?" Johnson asked, grinning.

"Ha! Factory floor! There is no one working on the factory floor anymore. It's all robots. That's the beauty of robots, they don't complain about management. Plus, there's no time off. They don't even need sleep. We reset them for an hour each month, disconnect the power, scan them for bugs and Trojan horses, then start them back up again... and off they go. The robots are still working as we speak: packaging food, preparing deliveries. They don't even need to go to the bathroom. They are fantastic. The best employees we've ever had. There's no need to pay them either," Conrad laughed.

Johnson rubbed his forehead. He didn't like to joke about job automations, all of them could be the next employees converted to digital. It was a slow moving inevitability.

"What time is it? Conrad asked.

Johnson looked up at the digital clock in the top corner of his wall screen. "It is exactly 20:25 and 15.75 seconds."

"Shit, the second half is nearly starting, I need to go to the toilet. Back in a sec," said Conrad.

Johnson went to his fridge and took out a beer, wishing today for something a little stronger. But wine was expensive, and he never drank spirits. He'd watched his father drink himself into a stupor after his mother died, and the smell of whiskey still haunted him.

He took a sip of his Eternal Sun Golden Ale, made with 'only the best ingredients – yeast, hops, barley, water and the strength and power of the sun'. It gave him a dull pleasure and set him down gently into the hazy present.

He sat back down on his couch and looked back at the main screen, at an ad for bottled water. He watched the perfect stream of 3D water rushing through a meadow and then off a mighty waterfall, straight into a bottle of Fresh2O.

The vision returned to the on-field camera. The field was covered with the icons and images of the companies that sponsored the sport. They crowded for coverage over the distant memory of the grassy-green field beneath. Some were animated cartoons, and some were three-dimensional with bubbled words that came right off the field, through the wall screen, clear and neat, into the lounge room of the viewer, reminding them sharply of their ever-changing needs.

As the players ran onto the field – the Capital City Chargers in the same red that adorned the vitamin bottles of their current naming rights sponsor, and the Amazon-Phizo Armadillos in black and white – one of the commentators spoke exuberantly over the top: "Both teams are no doubt eager to make it through tonight's Four Pillars Premiership match, where there is a considerable bonus on offer for a top-four finish. The winner of today's elimination final will also get automatic entry into the Global Club Challenge and a bonus of 800 million International Dollars."

The other commentator responded: "That's right, Nike. Great motivation right there. And the Vitastrength Chargers will need to turn things around quickly. The captain, ZMI Domingo, will need to lead from the front."

The first commentator jumped back in: "And they are really missing Kevlex out there. Word is that he has strained a ligament in his knee. And while the team doctors are regrowing one for him now, it is unlikely he'll be back tonight–"

Conrad reappeared. "Is the game on?" he asked. "My vision cut out, for some reason."

"It's on. The players just came back onto the field." The camera zoomed in on the NABOJ Trade Bloc banners – combining the defunct flags of the United States of America, Canada, Japan, Australia, New Zealand and Britain – and then the more common, unified flag with two triangles of red and blue meeting in the middle. "Have you linked up your HV again?" Johnson asked.

"I will now. I keep getting distracted by you," Conrad laughed. He was kneeling down as he spoke, and Johnson could only see the top of his blond hair. "Who's ordering the pizzas tonight?" he asked from his position on the floor.

"It's your turn, Conrad, and you should *slum* well know," Johnson exclaimed. Despite Conrad's usual protestations about paying, he eventually agreed to place the order. "Same as always for me," said Johnson, who ordered the ceroni, pineapple, synth-olive and hyped-onion pizza that he and his dad used to share.

For a moment, he forgot about the match being played out on his holo-vision screen and wondered how his father was going in his retirement home, and whether he'd ever get to see him again. Maybe when he is near the end, they might let me visit. "Bless him and the Economy," Johnson whispered to himself as he looked back to the big screen and his only real friend.

10.

Una walked up the long crumbling walkway. Either side of her, run-down tenements stood like old books crammed onto a shelf. Over the years, crude extensions and alterations had been haphazardly added to the buildings.

She took another step on the long, winding climb through the shanties. A pack of shirtless boys ran past her, kicking a football as they went. By the side of the walkway was a fruit and veg stall. An elderly lady stopped to survey the goods.

"How much for a bunch of bananas?" she asked. "Real ones!"

"Trade or buy?" asked the bearded vendor.

"Buy!"

The man rubbed his chin. "For you, love, a couple of gold coins will do."

Una was distracted by something that flew past her head. A wave of fear shot though her. *Was it a drone?* She glanced up and was relieved to see a bird flying between the tenements.

Una walked away from the stall and made her way down the rubbish-strewn street. She spotted the Green Emerald Café sign up ahead. The building was slightly newer than some of the other shops and stores on the busy Winding Way.

On reaching the café, Una ran her hand over the four-leaf clover stamped on the heavy wooden door. She knocked. There was no answer. She edged open the door and tentatively walked inside. It was dark, and for a moment the light from outside illuminated thousands of dust particles floating in the air. On the far side was an empty bar with stools. The door closed behind her, and the room was plunged into darkness.

Una heard a clicking sound. She could just make out a man sitting in the corner.

"Camus?"

He looked up from his LAN/S-pod. His face was slightly different from when she last saw him. But it was him, she could tell – as she always could with her comrades, despite Auntie Norma's best face changing work. It was funny that the facial recognition systems could not pick up the changes, but she could – as if she were sensing a part of their being beyond their faces.

He nodded, and then went back to typing.

"What are you doing here?" she asked.

"Trying to get the latest Renegade vision into one of the networks, get it into the RegNET," he answered without looking up.

"Any luck?"

"No, sadly. It has been blocked by all the main providers."

"Did anyone get to see it?"

"It's up on the dark web. But, as you know, that only gets to certain people..."

She sighed. "Our constant struggle."

"That's why we have to bring down the regulated internet," Camus whispered. "Open it up to the free flow of information."

"So the truth, our truth, gets out there," she added.

The door opened behind her. In the doorway was an elderly lady with long grey hair and a chubby, friendly face half-hidden under a purple felt hat. She was wearing a green cardigan and carrying a cotton bag. She walked across the room and dumped the bag on the counter.

The lady greeted Una warmly: "Welcome to the Green Emerald Café."

"You're Emerald, right," Una said as they shook hands.

"Yes, but you, my dear, can call me Eileen. Now, you look like you could do with a tea." Eileen walked over to the counter and turned on a kettle. "You must be hungry too?"

"No. I'm all good," Una replied, and then quickly added, "Do you know why Lenmar sent me here?"

"Let me just fix you a tea first, then we can get to why you are here," Eileen answered. She began looking inside a cupboard behind the bar. "Now where did I put the good stuff?"

Una sat down at one of the tables near Camus.

"Does he want a tea?" Eileen asked as she picked up a tin and an antique kettle from the 20th century. "What's he doing, anyway?"

"Trying to get some recorded footage back online," Una replied. She glanced across at Camus, who was glued to his computer screen.

"What's in the video? What's the message?"

"Lenmar's latest pleas for change, for people to rise up..."

"Sounds like the last one," Eileen said with a chuckle, before handing Una a mug of hot tea. "Any luck?"

Camus didn't respond. Una jumped in: "No, it's been blocked again."

Eileen put a hand on her shoulder. "We need to do something about that. Find a way to get it onto one of the big information providers and make sure these videos stay online for long enough to have an impact."

"How do you mean? Get inside or get access?"

"Access! Getting inside is the easy part, as you know," replied

Eileen. "But getting access to a network, and then making sure the content gets approved and put out to the world, well that's where you need an Information Editor."

Suddenly, the LAN/S-pod starting beeping, growing louder and louder. Camus flipped over the device and ripped out the batteries and memory card. He grabbed a sheet of electro-reflecto paper from the bar and frantically wrapped all the elements of the LAN/S-pod.

"Hornets!" he said, and then they were all frozen in silence.

11.

He looked up at the sky as he did every morning. It was bright blue from one horizon to the other, dotted here and there with huge advertisements – floating, rotating so they were always visible, following the eyes of the consumer below like a hypnotist with a pocket watch. Steel banners as big as 10 football fields sewn together, then bolted on to geostationary satellites with words painted in colossal letters that could be seen across the planet; words and symbols that advertised the multinational corporations and international conglomerates that could afford to buy the heavens. He could see them dotted across the sky: Amazon Global, The Marketplace, ABC Google, Creation Limited, Food Inc., Metscape, The Apple, Zhongcom, All-Mart, Anglo-American Finance, Globohold, Lylo Investments, Denseng, About-Face, P2, Hang-Tao... too many to name them all... and Johnson Goliath. He read his name written right alongside his brother's, in bold brown letters, high up in the sky above.

Johnson arrived at the tower and scanned his wrist at the employee entrance. There was a loud buzz as the doors swung open, and he walked inside.

"Welcome back, Employee Johnson – Information Editor."

Looming over the lobby was a hologram of a giant gorilla with the dark eyes and the bright-yellow banana smile. In the far corner, away from the lifts, was a reception room, where a robotic white desk welcomed visitors to Gorilla Industries.

Johnson thought he heard a squeaking noise from over in the reception area. Without thinking, he wandered over to the room and took a peek inside. He spotted an enormous man in dishevelled clothes sitting on a white leather couch. His large behind was moving around on the couch, making the squeaks. He was reading a book, which was a rare sight – most people spent their days glued to their tablets, PIDs or Eye-Tabs. Johnson could tell by his scruffy clothes that he wasn't an elite; they usually flew them in by hop-chopper to the tower roof. The man jotted down something in his book, and Johnson wondered if he might be an independent journalist or blogger, even one that had been reported for an information violation – though they probably didn't wait for them to visit, just sent the Company soldiers, guns in hand, straight to where the information had been uploaded to the web. Would there be a stern warning or an arrest for them? Or a bloodbath?

The reception entrance door slid open and a girl walked in. She was small, with tanned skin that looked soft to touch. Her big red hat and blue jacket reminded Johnson of a bear from a childhood book that his grandmother had read to him. The girl caught Johnson staring at her. He flushed red. She stopped in her tracks and seemed to be about to call out to him, when he bolted towards the lifts.

He breathed deeply and wiped the sweat from his brow. He had no business talking to clients or visitors. He shouldn't even be at reception. It was a direct breach of the Employee Regulations. But a part of him was intrigued, interested to know more. Who was she? And why was she there? But the chance had passed. She didn't look like an employee – she wasn't wearing the appropriate garb, and she walked with the freedom of the liberated.

After composing himself, Johnson pressed 165 into the digital pad by the lift. He hoped nobody had seen him dart across the lobby. It was a silly thing to do; he could easily have been scanned and reported to management.

On reaching his floor, he got out and walked to the Information Editing Unit. He saw Lylo across the room and gave a nod. Lylo nodded back, hir face stern as always.

He hesitated. "Nice morning out there," he said, as he glanced out the double-reinforced windows overlooking the western side of the Employee Village.

Lylo agreed, then went back to the screen.

Johnson shuffled across the carpet floor towards his desk, passing rows of separated cubicles, some with employees already seated and working, others empty with only the ghosts of those who had been let go. He looked over at the spot where Eileen used to sit and was hit by a wave of sadness for a better time. *Was it better?* he wondered. Or was he just being nostalgic for a time that had gone and could never come back? Work had been more enjoyable with her around, for sure, but it was still the same job, the same life – just another slave to the Company.

Once at his cubicle, he pushed aside the chair and adjusted the height of the desk so he could stand in front of it without leaning forward. It helped with the constant dull pain in his back, which was exacerbated by the long hours, the sedentary life and the constant pressure that seemed to close in from all sides. He reached down into his drawer and popped a canabanol tablet for the pain. He grabbed a Pep-Me-Up as well, and washed it all down with a bottle of H2GO that was sitting on this desk.

He pulled himself towards the double screen, scanned in, and placed his finger through the live DNA scanner. He opened up the system and began working slowly through his edits, going through a variety of vlogs and social media pages, making necessary adjustments and deleting unsavoury material.

There were a dozen controversial vlogs that had gone up on About-Face – it had its own channel that all the information providers were connected to, but Gorilla Industries still edited posts and geo-blocked unwanted profiles for any searches that came through the Gorilla Information Network.

As the day wore on, he started working on some further material for the Sunshine Retirement Homes content. The Motion Graphics Team had sent up a documentary-style film for review. He watched the footage of happy retirees enjoying the delights of their private Xanadu. Seeing their smiling faces as they walked through pine forests and past mountain lakes, he thought about his father in the Government-run retirement home, knowing that the only way his dad would get to see this kind of magic would be if they plugged him into Virtual Vision – and even that seemed unlikely, given how little money the Trade Bloc Government seemed to have for the elderly.

At that moment, a message came down from his manager, asking him to edit some recent growth data released by the School of Economics, with increases to the productivity and gross efficiency figures to be added prior to launching on the GIN.

There was a second message too, an urgent one asking him to help distribute, via all channels, a press release regarding increased anti-globalist activities in Capital City, and the threat that it brought to the Economy.

He felt a little uneasy. *What could that be about?* he wondered. He wrote back: *Sure. Is there some information from the Home*

Security Office to go with it? Any release data or footage that should be included?

There was a pause. He tapped his fingers on his desk, waiting, until he saw the reply being typed before his eyes: *Take whatever you have from the database. An old news story, some footage, whatever we've got.*

Who is this for?

A request from up top. It is urgent and needs to go out on all channels. Link it with some recent Sky-Fox news stories on the Food Inc. explosion. And then make sure it is primed for maximum impact. I don't want this one being lost in the ether.

Johnson looked at the press release and began reading:

The anti-globalist threat has been increased to 'mega-high' on the danger-alert chart. A new and genuine threat to the Economy by an underground anti-globalist group led by the malevolent masked tyrant known only as the Renegade, whose sole aim is the total destruction of the Economy. The Renegade will stop at nothing – and has no regard for growth, the rule of law, or the truth.

Johnson's face went white, wondering . He breathed out softly.

12.

"Recession free... Recession free... Recession free." The crowd continued to chant; their hands locked in prayer. "Recession free... Recession free... Recession free."

A plump man in purple robes walked to the front of the stage. He signalled for quiet. "Please bow your heads," he said as he looked down, his hands clasped together. A hush went around the auditorium. "We thank the Economy for staying strong, and the companies and businesses that allow it to grow. We hope for continued growth in the Economy, for inflation to rise steadily, and for employment and consumer confidence to stay high. We pray for the Economy to remain recession free."

Everyone repeated the last words, "Recession free" - this time in a more subdued fashion.

A skinny man wearing thick horn-rimmed glasses walked out on stage. He placed one hand over his other, clenched fist, pointed upwards, in salute. The priest returned the gesture.

"Thank you for that prayer, Priest Welsham." The skinny man gave the priest a tender tap. He raised his hands, calling for quiet. "Welcome to the School of Economics," he began. "As you are no doubt aware, I am Dean of the school." He paused. There were the sounds of people taking their seats. "Before we start, please put your Eye-Tabs and any other electronic devices on silent and turn off your microphones. We record these lectures, and they will be available online through the school website." He cleared his throat.

"And remember, if you want our economy to keep growing, we need to keep spending. And there is nothing better to spend your money on than an investment. If you are interested in investments, we have representatives of both Lylo Investments and The Finance Group here today. They will be available for questions at the end of the sermon. Or you can check them out online. There are links up on our website right now. All you need to do is click on the link and you can get an instant tutorial absolutely free." He paused for a moment and looked around the theatre. "Today's sermon is proudly brought to you by our partners at Lylo Investments, The Finance Group and Anglo-American Finance.

"For our guest lecture today, we have Angelique Gabrielle from the International Banking Confederation. She is going to talk to you about the importance of a steady rate of inflation. Welcome, Angelique." The Dean clapped as an elegant woman with short strawberry-blonde hair came out from behind a purple curtain to the side of the stage. She was dressed in a sharp grey suit and knee-high boots and walked with a swagger. Johnson recognised her from the news. He had heard her talking about the International Banking Confederation's weekly decisions on the cost of money and rates of exchange.

She stood before the lectern and spoke: "Thank you to the School of Economics for having me present today's sermon. It is a great pleasure to be here. The International Banking Confederation is always happy to share information about our first-rate economy.

"I am going to talk firstly about the continued deregulation of the banking and finance sector, which allows people like you and me the chance to invest in shares, options, futures, double futures and exchange portions. And then, at the end, I will talk about inflation and why a steady rate of inflation is integral to continued economic success within both the states and trade blocs and, more broadly, for the global community."

Johnson zoned out. He pressed a button on the side of his seat and a screen appeared underneath the glass 'food and drink' tray attached to the left of the seat. He ordered an MC^2 energy drink. A few minutes later, a small steel delivery-bot appeared before him with the can of 'liquid power' resting on a plate. He picked it up and sucked down a gulp with greedy satisfaction, feeling an immediate surge from the active ingredients contained within.

The drink immediately did its job – helping him to listen in to the lecture again, which seemed to go on and on, with the banking lady talking about deregulation and inflation, weaving the two topics in and out, always landing on a similar point about economic growth and financial success. He had heard it all before. But he didn't want a recession, nor did he want to lose his job, so he prayed with everyone else for growth. And he nodded as Angelique Gabrielle spoke ardently about keeping the banking industry free from rules and regulation – or 'red tape', as she called it, which, she said, would destroy all that people hold dear, making the purchase of food and clothes and gadgets all but impossible for regular consumers like him. But a part of him began to think of the words of that masked stranger, the Renegade, whose passionate entreaty against the system had sparked something inside him. And now he didn't shut them out, and now the words he heard in the School of Economics seemed orchestrated, as if designed by the elites and companies and shareholders for one sole purpose: to keep the system perpetually supportive of their own ends.

After the banker had finished her speech, the Head Priest

came back onto the stage and ended the sermon. He motioned with his hands, and everyone stood up and sang *Hark the Free Economy*. Johnson looked around at those singing, watching their faces intently; almost trying to catch a glimpse of the true feelings that may be hidden beneath their hearty singing. A few eyes turned his way, and he hurriedly joined in for the chorus:

Hark the free economy,
We are free to play and free to win, we are free to spend and free to be,
Oh hark the free economy... Oh hark the free economy.

Johnson filed out of the amphitheatre with everyone else. He was surrounded by all sorts of people: some were fellow employees he half-recognised from around the office or the Employee Village; others wore the uniforms of their varied employers; a few had dark sun-glasses and the serious stare of security guards; some were bunched in families, looking ragged and tired with children running around their feet; and others were refined and well dressed – possibly elites or property owners, but they normally held their own ceremonies away from 'the rabble'.

He heard his name shouted from behind. He turned and saw Raymond Melville – one of the few employees whose first and last names he knew. He remembered when they first met: Melville had held out his hand and confidently announced himself as Raymond Melville. It was odd, because most employees stuck with one name, and one employment position, as per Gorilla Industries standard. And preferably their new Company name if one had been taken or bestowed as part of an employment agreement. Gorilla had wanted Johnson to change his name when he started too, but in the end, it wasn't permitted by Johnson Goliath, who owned the rights to his name from a pre-existing contract signed by his parents when the school fees had been too much to bear; at a time when the companies were first signing up kids to sponsor. There had only been a few others in his school named directly after brands – a Keflex, an Adidas, a McDonald and a Bosch. Now, most people of school age had a sponsor, and the schools were filled with Apples and Mangoes and McDonalds and Lylos.

"How's your Sunday treating you?" Johnson asked, trying to sound as relaxed as possible, after they had greeted each other.

"Good, Johnson," replied Melville. "Are you heading back?"

"Yeah. I was about to leave."

"Great. We can head back together."

"Okay. That sounds good," said Johnson, feeling a little surprised by the invitation from a man with whom most of his interactions had been brief. "Is your family here?" Johnson asked tentatively.

"No. They couldn't make it." Melville replied. "My son is a bit sick at the moment."

"Sorry to hear that." Johnson did not want to pry and said nothing further as they headed away from the crowds.

Melville went on: "The kid has got some infection. It's totally resistant to antibiotics, of course, so he needs to be treated with superbugbiotics, but as you know, they have to be fed in by a drip."

"That sounds rough. I hope he'll be okay."

"I have been assured by the online doctor that he will be fine. They sent over a nurse with a drip. His mother is at home with him." He scratched at something beneath the grey hair on his head. "I have been told he should be right within a week," he smiled. "The miracles of modern medicine, hey, Johnson. Did you know that only 20 years ago my son would have died? Before superbugbiotics, this sort of infection was deadly. Nitzky, the Russian scientist who invented them, should be made an Ikea-Laureate."

"I do remember hearing about that at school, but I thought superbugbiotics were invented by the Kloonstek Corporation."

"That's what they want you to believe, Johnson," Melville winked. "Anyway, it is fascinating stuff. The basic antibiotic was all they had before Nitzky came along... and your friends at Kloonstek, of course. And, as you probably know, most infections are totally resistant to antibiotics."

"So, I guess we are lucky to be alive now," Johnson offered meekly.

"True! True! Of course, my son is very lucky. Anyway, enough morbid talk. Why don't we share a car?"

Johnson agreed, and they strolled together, side by side, towards the school's exit.

"I'll order it," Melville said as he pulled out an older-style tablet, moving his thumbs gracefully as he tapped at the screen. "Ah good! There's an electric car coming past here in four minutes."

They stood, waiting in an awkward silence that was only cut off by the arrival of the car.

"After you," Melville said. Johnson jumped into the back of the generic white car. Melville got in the front.

"Destination Gorilla Industries Compound, employee entrance. Please scan wrist chip to confirm," the voice-activated autopilot said as the doors closed. Melville scanned his wrist against the chip reader on the dashboard of the automated vehicle. Lights flashed in recognition. "Second passenger chip scan required," the voice added.

"You want to split the ride?" Johnson asked.

"No, I'll cover it."

"Thanks, Raymond." Johnson scanned his chip on the chip reader in front of him.

"Welcome, Passenger Johnson." It gave him the option to split the ride cost, which he declined. And they were off, shooting down the electric car-grid, with other cars and the odd truck or van passing them in all directions, missing them by inches but never looking like they would collide.

"It's a great invention," said Johnson as much to himself as Melville.

"What's that?" asked Melville.

"This car-grid. I remember the days before we had it. I mean, they always had the driverless car and Uber ridesharing... and terrible public transport," Johnson laughed. "But when they invented the car-grid, well it changed everything," he added, knowing there was a dark side too – for those blacklisted and banned from the grid.

"Ah yes," Melville said, "ABC Google's greatest ever achievement. Although if the news reports are right, they are about to create fully functioning artificial intelligence with a brain as independent and creative as a person, and an infinitely greater ability to learn."

"Really?"

"Looks like it. And not just the analytics and information of the old generative models."

"I guess that's pretty exciting," said Johnson. He didn't know much about the Brain Race, but he'd listened to Rachael tell him the basics. Even as an early prototype herself, she had mentioned some serious risks with its development. "But it's also a bit scary, don't you think?"

"You're telling me. Imagine a machine with the same drive to live as a person, and then it realises that the only way it could be shut down is by the very people that invented it. We are its only threat. And this machine could be a billion times smarter than the average person, with access to every piece of knowledge or information on the internet, everything ever recorded since the dawn of time."

"So, it would want to destroy the people that invented it?"

"It wouldn't want to Johnson. These machines don't have emotions. It would be like you pulling out a weed that was growing on the footpath near your house. It would just be a matter of course. To the machines, we may seem as irrelevant and unnecessary as that weed."

They drove on across town. There was silence for a while, which was broken by Melville, who began rabbiting on about the Information Editing Unit and the importance of Johnson's work for the Company and the Gorilla Information Network. Johnson listened, wondering how Melville knew so much about what he did. It made him a little wary, as if Melville was in some sort of position of authority. Johnson had even considered that he could be his manager - the infamous Information Manager that covertly set his daily tasks. If so, he would have received the Renegade's vision-stream, which he'd blocked and sent back, during the week, and was playing on this mind.

Johnson now considered asking Melville about the film: testing the water with a casual but obscure enough reference so he could cover his tracks... knowing a wrong word could be disastrous. He would face the sack if they knew his thoughts or of his desire to see and hear more. And that would mean the end of all he knew – of Rachael, his job, his safety and security, and his home in the village. And the thought of living out there, alone, in the slums, fighting for food and water as he sought other employment, was too frightening to consider. His name would go straight onto the employment 'blacklist' and none of the other big companies would hire him. So he kept quiet, kept his head down, did his job, and never pushed the boundaries with people like Melville.

They reached the compound. Both men jumped out of the car, which immediately shot off in search of other passengers. They stood a few yards before the enormous black metal barred gate. It was closed. Company soldiers stood at the side with two fierce-looking Rott-Shepherds prowling the perimeter. A security camera was attached to the top of the gate, with a security owl perched above, ready to take flight should there be trouble. It was said it was programmed to sense anxiety and would attack anyone who wasn't supposed to be there with its sharp steel talons.

Melville scanned his wrist at the identification checkpoint and then waited as his face was scanned by the Company soldiers. They were dressed in their yellow-and-brown 'Gorilla' fatigues. They looked ready for war with their guns and packs, loaded belts, heavy padded jackets and helmets. The gate unlocked with a jolt, and then a slow screech as it slid open. Melville darted through.

Johnson moved forward to be checked. He glanced up and saw the owl. It had turned around and was facing him, staring unblinkingly with its grey slit-like eyes, a lifeless and brutal machine ready to pounce, following his every move like the satellite advertisements followed everyone. He saw the lens-eye zoom in on his face. He turned away quickly, desperately hoping the owl hadn't sensed his terror. *Can it read my thoughts?* he wondered. Perhaps it had sensed his hesitation with the song at the School of Economics lecture, or his secret feelings about the Renegade film. Was the content he wrote for the Gorilla Network not good enough? Did he go too easy on the masked reactionary with the powerful voice and penetrating gaze? Forgetting, perhaps, for a moment, the man was anti-globalist. Or had he searched for the video stream in his drunken stupor the other night?

The gate remained closed, steadfastly refusing to buzz open. A soldier walked over slowly. *Will they let me in?* he wondered with growing anxiety, and the fear of being taken in for interrogation, or thrown to the wolves like the bald man and his old friend, Eileen? The soldier stood before the gate and stared him down. The gate clicked open, and the thickset beast moved towards him, taking up the entire gateway with his imposing presence.

There was the sound of a voice behind them, calmly calling out for the Company soldier, who stopped in his tracks and turned back. Melville was there. He walked up to the soldier with all the confidence in the world, warning him about some potential anti-globalist threat he'd spotted on route from the School of Economics. Johnson half-listened as he slipped through the gate and into the compound. He had no idea what Melville was on about – he hadn't seen anything much on their car ride, let alone an attack or even an anti-globalist... whatever they looked like.

13.

Una sat on the couch, waiting. In the adjoining room was her friend, getting a new face. It would be Una's turn next.

The door opened. Mallaroy walked out. Her skin was still dark, but her cheeks and lips seemed thinner – the magic of Auntie Norma. Her hair had been straightened too and was tied at the back. She was wearing thin grey glasses instead of the usual, black-rimmed monstrosities.

"Looking 'good', Mallaroy."

"It is Parks now," replied her friend, "only Parks."

Una nodded solemnly, noticing her friend's new teeth. The front ones were now almost bucked, with a gap that had been opened up in the middle or chiselled away, as was usually the case.

"I like it," said Una. "It has a nice ring to it."

"Me too – I feel a connection to the real Rosa Parks."

"I can see that," Una said with a laugh. She stood up, took a step towards Parks and examined the changes. "It looks so real," she added as she gently touched her friend's cheek.

Parks moved her head back slightly as if trying to protect her new face. "Yeah, it is a good one. Auntie Norma is a wonder."

"How's your grandmother?" Una asked. "She on board?"

Parks nodded. A tear appeared in her eye. 'She is, which is great, but you know, also terrible."

Una nodded. 'I understand,' she said, touching Parks gently on the shoulder, wanting to embrace her properly.

There was an awkward pause, before Parks went on: "Anyway, I've got to get going... before its time. I'll see you later."

"Hopefully," Una replied with affection, but there was also a hint of concern in her voice. They hugged. Una kissed Parks softly on the cheek. It might be the last time they saw each other – it was always like that for them. Despite Park's tough, cold exterior, there was warmth below the surface, which was hidden from most, but not her. It helped when they had given up so much – their families, everything.

A loud buzzing noise came from the door. Parks took the cue and left, their eyes meeting for a moment. Una headed over to the room. It was her turn to get a face, a new one to go over the original, whatever that was – she gave that up when she joined the cause. But in a way she also gained it back...

She opened the door and entered the room. It was small. Before her was a large paint-flecked mirror. Underneath was a dressing table covered with make-up and plastic tubs of glue. One entire wall was cut up into white shelf-like boxes filled with a variety of prosthetic faces, wigs and skin, and malleable silicone flesh.

"Come on in, Una, and take a seat," said Auntie Norma, putting her customary glass of whiskey down on the dressing table.

Una sat down in a quaint 20th-century hairdressing chair. Auntie Norma swivelled her around with heavy shoulders, like a human farmer moving hay bales before the automations.

"Now I know you only like small changes," Auntie Norma said as she trotted over to the dressing table.

"Yeah, I still want to be able to see myself in there," Una replied.

"Just enough to beat the facial recognition system, hey?"

'Yeah, but I also need to look a bit like this,' Una said as she pulled out the picture and unfolded it.

Auntie Norma picked up the image. 'Digital, hey?'

Una nodded. 'That's what the guy told me.'

'I can do that,' Norma said with a grin, as she grabbed hold of a small skin fuser. Una grimaced, wishing she didn't have to go through it all again.

"Now don't worry," said Auntie Norma with a wink, "she looks good, and not so different from you.'

Una was not so sure. Changing her face was one thing, a necessary part of her job, but trying to look like someone else was getting a little extreme. As Auntie Norma prepared her chin with pre-fuse, she began to consider her new name.

14.

The lunch bell rang, blasting him from his thoughts like an alarm, reminding him of the time. He grabbed his small shoulder bag, with his pills and bottle of water, and looked around. His colleagues in the Information Editing Unit were unmoved. Many stayed at their desks at lunchtime – ordered delivery and watched a movie or searched the web – but Johnson liked to get out to the cafeteria.

He headed to the employee lift and jumped aboard. The lift was empty, save for the cameras and the digital presenter on the wall, which began squawking the latest celebrity gossip at him as soon as the door closed: *"Fantasy Music legend Gotrella Martinez has received the People's Popularity Award for the third month running..."*

"Switch to news," ordered Johnson, and the screen flicked over to footage of Creation Limited HQ with its famed Bodhi tree out front.

"Creation Limited, which specialises in re-creating after-life and virtual reality experiences, is developing a new product named Life. The program – in which an entire life can be lived in virtual reality, with all personal choices and life occurrences programmed in prior to entering the system – is set to be released shortly, with expectations that it will break the record for highest-grossing game of all time."

"Its release has been indefinitely delayed in the Eurozone, with the European Commission concerned that the new program will fall foul of

its Charter of Difference requirements. Creation Limited has already flagged its intention to take the matter to the International Trade Court, with the full backing of NABOJ. Chief Executive Hope confirmed that, saying, 'The Eurozone's continued attempts to block our businesses from accessing their markets will be met with full economic might.'"

"In refugee news, thousands of refugees continue to move from North Africa, attempting to illegally bypass the Iberian fence, into the Eurozone and then on into the NABOJ Trade Bloc."

Johnson caught a glimpse of the footage as he departed the lift. There was a giant black metallic fence running into the distance, with a mass of scrawny dejected-looking migrants pushing up against it, some attempting to climb and then dropping off like cake-crumbs as they hit the electrified zone. He exited the lobby, feeling sad for those millions of African refugees trying desperately to outrun the encroaching desert and year after year of failed crops. But what could he do? The only ones with the power to do anything were the trade blocs and the multinationals, and the International Banking Confederation, of course – but they just seemed to argue about inflation and loans, as they kept everyone beholden to the International Dollar.

He moved on towards the courtyard and then turned immediately left, following a scattered line of fellow employees heading the same way. He walked by the side of the tower block and then back in at the end, arriving at the main cafeteria – an enormous space, like a school hall, with a cream-coloured vinyl floor. There was a counter at one end, and hundreds of small, round silver tables with only one or two chairs at each.

Johnson reached a long metallic counter. Behind it, four bots moved along a track, taking orders and then scooting off to the food platters.

There was a fairly broad range today: a mix of stews, crumbles and tasties, some pasta, flavoured rice, artificial salads, the usual chicken and fish options, roasted or chipped vegies, and a variety of other dishes. Johnson ordered the jacket potato with mushed tuna, sweet corn and mayonnaise. It was laboratory tuna, of course. There was no way to get natural tuna; after the oceans had been fished out of smaller fish, the tuna had followed, and were now pretty much extinct in natural form – at least that is what he'd read online.

The lunch-bot arrived with his meal. Johnson swiped his wrist for payment as the tray of food was released into his possession. He walked to the refrigerated vending machine by the wall and ordered a low-GI ginger beer.

He flopped down on a lone seat at one of the round metal tables and gazed admiringly around the giant hall. Other employees sat, eating quietly. Some were looking out at nothing, their heads moving slightly to the side, a dead giveaway that they were logged on to their Eye-Tabs.

Johnson grabbed his bag off his shoulder and took out four small containers. He put them beside him. They were full; he'd received this latest supply only last week, dropped on his doormat at the front of his house in exchange for last month's empties. They said this was to recycle the containers, but he wondered if they were checking up, making sure he was taking his full allocation – a backup to the weekly blood tests. He didn't know if the other employees had the same as him – they had analysed his physical, psychiatric and emotional wellbeing when he started the job, and his first medicinal supplements had arrived a few days later – but he'd seen enough of them taking out their own bottles and ingesting similar-looking tablets to know that he wasn't alone. What they got, he didn't know, but then he wasn't entirely sure what he got either, apart from the Pep-Me-Up pills. He knew them, because he'd been taking them since high school, and they had the infamous 'pep' logo carved into the top in tiny letters.

He tapped out a brown tablet from the taller, yellow vial. It was bigger than the others. He assumed from the earthy, metallic taste that it was a vitamin supplement of some sort. Then there were the tranquilium anti-anxiety tablets; and the fourth, he had no idea, but every time he had one, he felt a wave of enthusiasm for his work at Gorilla Industries.

Johnson took out one of the 'feel-good' tablets, as he called them, and looked it over. He nearly put it in his mouth, but then held off. He wondered if the feel-goods were distorting his thinking, maybe dampening things. He was about to put the pills away in his bag, but then changed his mind and grabbed a Pep-Me-Up. *Just to get me through the afternoon.*

He ate a chunk of potato and double-blinked his Eye-Tab back on. "Hello Rachael," he whispered.

"Hi Johnson," she replied, as if she had been expecting his call at that very instant. "How can I be of service?"

"I'm just calling in about dinner tonight."

"Go ahead."

"I was thinking of having a burger."

"I like your choice," she said. "Do you want a Beef-o, chicken, lentil, vegetable or mushroom patty?"

"I think I'll have a Beef-o burger, with salad." He paused. "Oh, and a side of hot chips, sauce-infused," he added as he tapped his stomach, feeling a twinge of guilt, knowing he needed to do more than the odd virtual boxing session.

"Your order has been placed with Mega-Menu and will be delivered at 21:00, with a three-minute variable depending on the weather. Please advise if you will be late home from work so the delivery time can be changed."

"Okay, thanks," he said.

"Did you know that Beef-o was the first pseudo-meat invented?" Rachael asked as he took another bite of his lunch.

"That sounds like another one of your facts, Rachael," he laughed, appreciating the education feature that he'd once programmed into her being.

"I love Beef-o, but I don't think I ever got to eat the real meat," he added, thinking back – unless his mother had cooked it when he was too young to remember, or he'd had it at his auntie's farm, but it must have slipped from his memory, like so much of that time. He didn't really know much about cows or beef either, and asked Rachael to give him some more information.

She obliged, telling him that cows were commonly farmed throughout the world for both meat and milk but, eventually, due to the costs associated with farming – water and carbon costs, as well as the extraordinary amount of grain that cows consumed – most people stopped eating them.

"Just like that?" he probed.

"It took some time. The price went up, they added consumption taxes, and eventually they put limits on the number of cows each state and trade bloc could breed, and then set maximum thresholds of feed per cow and a maximum age of 200 days. This is why beef became such a rare commodity."

Some of what she told him sounded familiar – learned at school or on the web. "So that was when they invented Beef-o?" he asked.

She briefly explained the history of Food Inc. and its development of Beef-o, and then Genoma developing a whole host of synthetic foods in response.

He thanked Rachael for the information, blinked her off, and provided a four-star review, as per the advice of his online support tool, which stated that artificial intelligence units were like dogs and worked better with reward over punishment.

After he finished his meal, he returned his tray to the automated cleaning section. As he walked out of the cafeteria hall, he saw a girl with dark-brown hair, cut short like a mushroom – he wondered if it was the same person he'd seen arriving at the reception area of Gorilla Industries, with the red hat. It couldn't be. He looked closer at her face. She looked like Rachael – although he saw her in all the girls he liked. She was at a far table, talking to Raymond Melville. Seemingly deep in conversation. She sat neatly with her legs to the side. He wondered what she was doing talking to him. He almost went over to Melville in the hope of being introduced – especially now that they had shared a ride home from the School of Economics – but talking to girls was not his strong point. He decided he'd better get back to work. Plus, his hour was nearly up, and he didn't want to get fined. The fine for coming back late from lunch was too big, cut too much into his weekly pay packet. It was not worth it. Still, he smiled at her as he left.

She looked straight at him and smiled back.

He felt euphoric, filled with a combination of amatory elation, and energy from the Pep-Me-Up pill, which was just kicking into gear... right on time.

PART II

1.

He is squashed inside a metal cage, his head thumping with pain. He can feel something in his eye. His hands are cuffed, so he wipes his face against the side of the van. It is blood, mixed with dirt, thickened up like toothpaste. He must be cut, over the eye, where it stings.

Opposite him, the police soldiers are sitting on a bench that runs down one side of the van. It is dark, but he can still see them. They sit rigidly with automatic rifles between their legs. They wear helmets, dark goggles and puffed-up bulletproof jackets; dressed ready for war.

"Where am I going?" he mumbles.

They sit like stone, cold and unmoved. *Are they even human?* But then he remembers the knee in his back as he lay on the ground – it was flesh and bone, not steel and silicone.

"Please tell me," he adds, looking up at them, pleading.

One soldier turns his way and grunts. It is all he gets. He wonders where they are taking him. Worst of all, he is deflated by failure. Any chance to find Maya is over. She is lost, gone without hope.

He screams out. Pained anguish wades through him. It has all become too much. He closes his eyes, trying desperately to find a place where he can be free of the pain, away from this world and all the horror within. He wishes, for a moment, that he still had his Eye-Tab and could forget it all and dive headlong into the digital world; that he could still have that choice.

His muscles are cramping from the tightness of the cage, his wrists cry out in pain from the handcuffs. Fear and helplessness have enveloped his being. Paralysing thoughts close in on him from every direction like Rain Maker storm clouds. Thoughts he can hardly deal with now – about his father, and that unspeakable horror of which he has just learned, and Maya... always Maya.

2.

She stood before him in the cafeteria, a lunch tray in her hands. She was beautiful, cute like a doe but sensual. The short, dark hair and honey-brown complexion was as he remembered. Her face reminded him of a full moon, the naturally occurring one, but there was also Rachael there too. She had a small frame, unlike Rachael, and what looked like strong legs, beneath her grey slacks.

"Can I sit here?" she asked.

Johnson looked up. "Um, em..."

"I'd really like to."

"Yes, of course," he said, slowly regaining his composure.

She sat down opposite him. Her skin looked soft and he wanted to reach out and touch it. He had not touched a *real* woman for so long – it was hard to remember what it felt like, what they felt like. When he was desperate for the touch of a woman, he put on his Virtual Vision, scrolled through the options, and then made love to a hologram – usually Rachael. Virtual sex was a pleasant way to pass the evening, but it was nothing like being with a real woman. With the real Rachael there had been electricity: something happened when the tips of his fingers rubbed across her cheek, or back, something undefinable, something that could not be replicated by his virtual reality headset. And now a real woman sat before him, looking directly at him, into him.

"Didn't I see you once before?" the girl asked.

"Yes, I think so. I saw you, I mean," he stammered.

She tilted her head to the side. "Really?" She began searching him over with her big, brown, chocolate eyes.

"Well, yes. Here, once before. A few days ago, I think."

"Yes, that's right. You smiled at me."

Johnson was relieved that she remembered.

"Why did you smile at me?" the girl said suddenly.

"I don't know." He looked down at his near-empty plate of food.

"That's not much of an answer." She was staring at him.

After a long pause, he looked up and said, "I thought you were pretty."

"That's nice. I remember you too. You walked out as I sat down for my interview."

"An interview for what?" he asked excitedly.

"A job, silly," she responded, smiling, one arm on her hip, the other resting on the table.

"Here?"

"Of course, here! Where else?"

"I didn't think you worked here. You're not wearing the uniform." Johnson looked around; the room was filled with his colleagues in their grey or navy shirts with a thin yellow line down each side, and the infamous Gorilla logo over the breast pocket.

"They haven't given me my uniform yet," she said softly. "Not that I want I really want one," she added, almost whispering. 'But it looks almost the same, doesn't it?'

Johnson nodded. 'I guess.' He ate another one of his bite-sized hash browns. "What department are you in?"

"You will have to guess that," she said. "But I will give you a clue," she added, her eyes sparkling.

Johnson nodded excitedly.

2.

"Let's just say it involves research."

"That's easy,' Johson shot back. 'Research and Development."

She shook her head. "No, similar but not quite."

"Science and Research?"

"Well, sort of. We do scientific research and testing for companies and send that information on to the right channels for release on the network."

"What's the department called?" he probed.

"I can't say." She winked. "But let's just say, I work in the laboratory."

"I didn't even know we had one."

"Well, where do you think the Research Department gets their information?"

"I suppose," he replied.

She took another bite of her sandwich. "Where do you work?"

"I'm in the Information Editing Unit."

"And what do you do there?"

"We edit any online material uploaded to the network channels; make sure it accords with the standards and values of Gorilla Industries."

She looked at him with a passive, almost bored, expression.

"And I create new content," he added, "for companies seeking web articles, news vids, opinion pieces, social posts, whatever is needed, then we load them up to the Gorilla Information Network, get them spiralling out so they get picked up by the algorithms and stay relevant."

"That sounds interesting," she said.

"Yeah, and sometimes I use scientific research that gets sent up to me for those promotional articles and paid content... so maybe I get that from you."

"Well, I've only been here a few days, so maybe not yet, but it sounds about right. Anyway, enough work talk. I am starving and I'm going to *try* to eat this." She nodded at her sandwich. "What do you think it is?"

"I don't know," Johnson laughed. "It looks like synth-cheese, and not sure what that red thing in there is – ceroni maybe?"

She winced. "Something made in a laboratory, no doubt. With no nutritional value at all." She giggled. "Which I guess is to be expected here at this awful café."

Johnson looked around to make sure no one was listening. Criticising the canteen was a direct violation of the employee code of conduct. "You want one of these?" he murmured, pushing his tray towards her, offering up his last hash brown.

"No. Let's go eat somewhere else."

"What, now? I can't… I mean, sorry, I would love to, but I have to get back to work," he stammered, regretting the words before they had even tumbled out of his mouth. But what choice did he have – he couldn't just leave, no matter how much he wished.

She looked at him pitifully, then shrugged her shoulders. "Fine!"

Johnson felt the moment slipping away. "Well, what about another day?" he blurted out, forgetting his usual reserve.

"I thought you'd never ask." She twirled the back of her hair with her index finger. "Saturday, in the evening, would work. What time do they *let* you finish?"

"I finish early on Saturdays, around 17:00. We could meet after that," he suggested, his hands jittering nervously.

"Alright, sounds like a plan. I'll meet you out the front."

"You mean at the employee entrance, at the back of the compound?"

"At the back of the compound?" she repeated, her mouth hanging open. "Now why would I want to go there?"

"Sorry, that's just where I normally go out. It's where I live," he answered, his voice softening. "Don't you live there?"

"Let's meet at the front," she said forcefully. "Right outside on the street, after you finish work... and then we can go into town and have a real meal, with real food."

Johnson sat for a moment, stunned, as it dawned on him that he had a date with a real girl – a beautiful and intriguing girl, the likes of which he'd never come across before. And certainly not like this, at work, with *her* coming up to *him* and demanding to be taken out. It felt surreal, like something out of an HV drama.

"So it's settled then?" she probed, some strands of brown hair flopping forward over her eyes.

"Yes, it sounds great," he said with such enthusiasm that he thought, for a moment, he may have spoiled the whole thing.

She shrugged. "Well, I'm going to be off then, because I can't eat any more of this." She threw down her half-eaten sandwich with exaggerated effect. "I will see *you* on Saturday." She pointed at him with a teasing finger. "Don't work too hard this week. I don't want you tired for our date." She turned away.

"No, I promise I won't," he replied heartily, before remembering the cameras and microphones that were everywhere in the cafeteria. He looked around. There was a set of cameras hanging from the ceiling about 20 metres away, probing the room for reportable offences. He wondered if the attached microphones had picked up what he said and sent it to the security department. "Sorry," he whispered to the air, not really knowing if that would do any good.

She turned back to him. "What's that?"

"Oh nothing," he replied, somewhat sheepishly. "Nice to meet you…" He realised he didn't even know her name.

"Maya!" she exclaimed.

"I'm Johnson."

"Oh, I know who you are, Johnson," she replied mysteriously.

He was taken aback. "Did you scan me before?" he asked.

"Of course! I had to know who you were before coming over here. I don't just go out on dates with anyone."

It was a date! His heart sang.

3.

He arrives and climbs out of the car, twisting his back slightly as he gets out. It hurts a little; an odd pain he's never felt before. It feels almost like a clunk, if a pain could be a sound, but he ignores it, for now, and closes the car door with a clang. There is no need to say thanks – there is no driver. It has all become automated in recent years. The Pharmagold '5 Star' Hospital is before him. It is more of a hospice than a hospital; a place for the terminally ill to come and wait for death to arrive, replete with a constant supply of Pharmagold pain medications.

Johnson tossed and turned in his bed; the Dream Weaver electrodes attached to his head, the cables crisscrossing the starched sheets.

He trots through the entrance, past Security, to the lift. It takes him to the fifth floor. He strides down the corridor, turning where he needs to, not even bothering to sign in at reception. He knows where he's going now, he's been here enough times. They let him through without question; they know him too.

He reaches the room and pulls aside the curtain. She is asleep, her body propped up by a mountain of pillows. She lays there, unmoved, the drip in her arm connected to the machine by her bed. His dad is there, in the same chair – the faded blue comfy one in the corner. He sits still, looking only at her. His eyes are red, as if he's been crying. Johnson nods to his father. His father looks up from his daze, pauses as he recomposes himself, and then greets him warmly, more warmly than is necessary. He looks tired. What is he doing? Coming to this place every spare moment of his day, sleeping in that chair each night. He's even taking days off work to see her, and then spending all day here, sitting by her bed, staring – staring at a shell.

How is his father affording this? he wonders. It must be bankrupting him. And for what? There will be no miracle. The cancer is in her blood, constantly circulating through her entire being, killing her, one atom at a time. He almost wishes she would go quickly, to end the pain, to end her slow demise. The cost of keeping her here each day, in a premium hospital like this, must be destroying his father's last savings... the cancer is killing them both.

He grabs the flimsy plastic seat at the side of the bed and pulls it close. He takes his mother's hand in his and looks into her eyes. They are dull; have lost their life force from the cancer and the morphine, and whatever else they pump into her body. He feels her grip, a gentle squeeze. He squeezes back. He leans forward and kisses her on the top of the head. "I love you, Mum," he says.

4.

Johnson stood at the entrance to Gorilla Industries. He was tired, struggling for air, after leaving out the back through the Employee Village exit, passing through the security of the Company soldiers and the mechanical owl, hoping they wouldn't turn on him, then walking the entire mega-block of the compound. He'd been too scared to walk through the reception area and out the front door. It was a no-go zone for employees, and a rule he wasn't yet ready to break.

He sucked in a gulp of fresh air and then began to take note of his surroundings, painting it into existence by his awareness. The sun was out, and it warmed his skin. The sky was clear of clouds but dotted here and there with satellite advertisements that coloured the blue like a host of kites in the days when kites were legal – before the number and value of commercial drones had forced a ban on anything that flew unregistered in the air, including birds.

It is nice to be out, he thought, realising how little he left the compound, apart from the odd School of Economics sermon on a Sunday.

He stood against the building wall. Beneath the giant, almost fierce-looking Gorilla Industries logo, the wall was blindingly white, to allow consumers to paint it with whatever colours or art they fancied through the Banksy App on the Eye-Tab. Above him hung the canopy. It was blue and arched its way along the building, about five metres off the ground. Nearly every building had one. They were made of reinforced steel, designed to be a stylish architectural addition to the building's façade, but everyone knew their real purpose: when an employee got sick of the grind and jumped off the roof or out an unsecured window, they stopped the body from reaching the pavement, protecting the people below from raining men and women, and the unsightly mess they created – and the contagion of suicide.

He looked up and down the street, searching for Maya. All he saw was a clean, lifeless street with high-rise buildings on either side. He could see Amazon Global's Capital City Compound, the Denseng Headquarters, the Lylo Building, a Mega-Menu dispatch and a few other, unmarked towers. And then there was the concrete fortress, square and foreboding, with cameras on all sides. He wasn't sure if it was a NABOJ Trade Bloc building or a branch of the International Banking Confederation – both organisations were notoriously secretive.

There was no sign of his date. He put his hands in his pockets, moving up and back along the footpaths like a tiger in a poorly designed enclosure. He looked left and then right, towards the pedestrian bridge that ran over the road by the Denseng Headquarters. Underneath, white vehicles on the car-grid zoomed past. Johnson headed up onto the bridge but couldn't spot her.

He walked back slowly. Perhaps she had forgotten or didn't want to see him. He was a fool to think a beautiful girl like her could truly desire his company.

"I'll give her 30 seconds," he said to himself, and then began counting. By the time he reached 20, he slowed so that each second took two or three seconds to complete. By the time he hit 29, he was counting so slowly that it seemed he may be stuck there for eternity.

"Hello Johnson."

He turned to see Maya standing before him. He opened his mouth and was about to mention how long he had waited, but her beaming smile made it all worthwhile, as if the lateness itself was now part of her charm. She was wearing an olive-green cardigan and white three-quarter-length pants. The white of the pants contrasted nicely with her honey-brown skin.

"I hope you haven't been waiting too long," she said. "I didn't even know the time." Before he had a chance to answer, she grabbed him by the arm. "Let's go," she said, and whisked him down the street. It felt good. Johnson didn't want her to let go.

"I'll order a car," said Johnson.

"No. Let's catch a train," replied Maya.

"A train?"

"Yes, the underground trains. I love them. I love rumbling along a track, through a tunnel, imagining what's above me, what part of the city I'm under as we fly along."

"Righto! Where is the station around here then?" he asked. "I don't remember the last time I caught a train."

"There is a station not too far from here," she said, "Commercial Centre it's called, and it's just across there... and ah, down there." She pointed to a street on the other side of the road. As she led him back to the pedestrian bridge, a swarm of delivery bees took off from the Mega-Menu dispatch and zoomed off across the sky.

The pair crossed the bridge and, after a short walk, reached a big open square area. Maya pointed to a tall building across the other side. "That's the Data Collection Bureau," she said. "Where they auction off harvested data."

Opposite where they stood, there was a small sign with an image of a yellow train and 'Commercial Centre' written across the top. He followed her down some clunking escalators in need of repair, and along a long white tunnel with yellow-and-white tiles. Faded advertisements adorned the walls, some for companies that had long gone out of business.

A busker stood in the corner, playing his violin. His face was dirty and his clothes grey and ragged, but his magical fingers skipped up and down the fingerboard with ease. Maya stopped to listen to the haunting, melancholic music. Maya opened her handbag and gave the busker something wrapped in tissue. The man nodded, his eyes meeting hers for an instant, before he went back to his violin.

There's nothing I can give him, thought Johnson. His money was all linked to his wrist chip. There were no coins, no notes, no tangible money anymore. He'd used banknotes as a kid, but he could barely remember what they looked like.

"What did you give him?" he asked as they walked away.

"Ah, just something he can actually use," Maya replied, refusing to say more.

They reached the end of the corridor and turned down some stairs. Johnson looked back. He thought he saw the ragged busker put something in his mouth and then wash it down with a bottle of foul-looking reddish liquid.

"Come on," shouted Maya, "or we'll miss the train."

Johnson followed Maya down the stairs, where they came upon a platform with train tracks on either side. The platform was scattered with people, a few chatting, most watching their Eye-Tabs or reading info on their PIDs while they waited for the train.

"This way goes into town," she pointed down the tracks. "And the other side heads to the outer suburbs and then around to the port."

"I've never been to the port," said Johnson.

"Ah, you must," Maya responded. "It's beautiful, looking out at the sea – millions of miles of empty blue ocean, and fish and other strange creatures hidden deep beneath the waves. It's where we came from, the water, millions of years ago... so that's why it always feels nice to be there."

Johnson felt a rush of hot wind as a train appeared out of the darkness of the tunnel. It came to rest at the platform. They jumped aboard. The doors hissed shut, and the train raced off at high speed. He wondered if it was safe. There was only a few centimetres' difference between following a nice, neat line under the city and hurtling into a rocky wall. He hoped the track was maintained better than the escalators in the station. He looked at Maya. She was staring out the small carriage-door window. The tunnel lights flashed magically across her brown eyes.

"Where are we going?" he asked.

"Wherever we want to go. But firstly, I think we should go here." She pointed at St Gates on the map above the door. "There's a park near there that's nice to walk around."

Passengers came and went at the stations. A family got on with two children. They sat down across four seats, the children unmoved, opposite their parents. One was locked into his Eye-Tab, concentrating on the data on his retina, his head moving with the action. The other, a little girl of about four with curly blonde hair, pulled out a Portable Internet Device and began watching a kid's show. Johnson peered over at the animated images bouncing across the screen – a giraffe, lion, rhino, and other creatures that had once roamed the savannas of Africa but had long since been extinct, beyond the zoos, where they competed for interest with genetic hybrids put together in test tubes by Denseng and others.

They arrived at their stop and hopped off. Johnson followed Maya as she headed up the stairs. Maya flicked a white card against the electronic gate and then darted through, while Johnson came behind, scanning through the usual way with his wrist chip. A few moments later, they were both standing out on the street. Johnson surveyed the scene and sucked in a gulp of fresh air.

"The park is over there," said Maya, pointing across the road. There was a small fountain in the centre, and Johnson immediately recognised the place. He had been there once before with his family when his mother had been sick in hospital. They had taken her out for a walk and come to this very park, which meant the hospital was close by. His brother had been there that day, before he'd joined the Home Security Office and they'd lost touch. He remembered it being pleasant, loving, despite the trying circumstances. Maybe his family's last good day together.

Maya and Johnson walked around the fountain square, the sun setting behind them. He told her about his mother and their day at this very park. They had eaten hot dogs and ice cream, and his mum had laughed, despite the pain from the cancer ravaging her frail body. She had been full of life that day, had dragged herself out of bed, as if her body was willing itself into this final act.

Maya listened attentively; her eyes almost magnetised to his as he told the story. They sat down at the fountain and enjoyed the silence for a few minutes. Johnson felt close to Maya as they sat side by side, their bodies near enough for their clothes to be touching and for Johnson to feel the warmth emanating from her body.

Darkness began to take hold, and the crowds in the park dispersed. 'Let's go for dinner,' Maya suggested. "I know this great Italian place not far from here," she said. "With pasta that is truly divine. Do you like pasta, Johnson? Of course you do, everyone does." She gave his arm a gentle squeeze.

They walked up a busy street to the main mall and jumped on a travelator running up between bars, restaurants and fashion boutiques. Johnson had never set foot in any of the shops they passed by, but he recognised the names. The mall was dotted with screens showing a loop of advertisements on repeat. The ads were in sync so it looked like they were dancing with one another, like fire demons, across the mall. One, which caught his attention, had footage of new-age animals fighting on the dirt floor of a small, round colosseum. A voice shouted over the images: *"Get you and your family down to the Eden Animal Arena next Saturday night for the best in genetically modified animal fights, including a liena and a leowolf in an all-out war, and the battle royal between Genoma's Land Shark and the undefeated Crocosauraus."* At the end of the footage, a white protestor-warning sign appeared on a black background, with a new, heavy-toned voice advising: *"Any protestors intending to attend or disrupt this event will face the full consequences of the Anti-Disruption and Protest Laws. With a minimum penalty of 15 years in prison."*

He stared at the screen, reminded of his one and only visit to the Eden Animal Arena. Gorilla Industries had taken the entire Information Editing Unit to watch, as part of a bonding session to boost morale after another round of ruthless layoffs.

He remembered the awful smell, the horror of the animals as they fought for their lives, and the sandy floor stained with blood at the end.

"Disgusting," said Maya.

"What, the animal fights?"

"Yeah, and the Protest Laws."

The images on the advertising screens cut to footage of a high-walled prison, and a soft female voice declaring: *"Globohold holds our most dangerous criminals, keeping them off the streets so you can feel safe. To help support our private prison system–"*

"Let's jump off here," Maya said as she nudged him down the exit ramp.

They turned off the main drag and headed down an alley filled with smaller bars and restaurants. They passed by a tall Gothic building. Johnson stopped, amazed by the high turret, intricate archways, wooden doors, and beautiful stained glass showing images of hallowed men and women surrounded by angels.

"What's that building?" he asked.

"It's a church," she replied. "I think it's an old Christian church."

Johnson shook his head in disbelief. "Wow, I read about them in school, but I've never actually seen one."

She laughed. "Really! Well, there are lots still left in the Latin Territories, but not so many here. Not now anyway."

"It's a nice building," he said, realising how much better it looked than the skyscraper monstrosities that towered over much of the city.

She agreed, saying something about the beauty found in everything.

4.

They continued down the street, the overhead lights thinning out as they went. And for the first time in a while, he glimpsed a star piercing the veil of the night sky.

Maya stopped as they came upon a green gate. Inside was a courtyard with some tables and chairs. A garden ran along the fence, and in the middle was a big willow tree with long, viny leaves that draped between the tables. The tables were covered with red-and-white chequered tablecloths, and simple round vases with flowers flopping over the side. In the corner, a man was gently strumming a guitar to the sway of the willow tree.

A tall, skinny man rushed out of the restaurant towards them. He had a moustache and long black hair slicked back in a ponytail. He wore a crisply ironed white shirt, a black vest over the top, and matching black pants. He smelled of garlic and basil with a hint of tobacco. He looked warmly at Maya, his hands outstretched towards her. "Ah, how wonderful to see you, Madam. But forgive me, for I have forgotten your name."

"Maya," she said.

"Yes, Maya, of course. How silly of me."

"At least I remember your name, Miguel. It's been so long since I've seen you. How are you?"

He laughed. "I'm always good," he said. He spoke in a thick Italian accent. "It's fantastic to have you here at the restaurant again, Maya." He bowed slightly. "You will be having dinner?"

"Of course," Maya replied. "Why else would we come," she added, her eyes sparkling.

Johnson introduced himself, holding out his hand tentatively.

Miguel stood there. He didn't move for a few seconds, then wiped his brow with his tea towel.

Maya ended the awkward silence: "Sorry, yes, Miguel, this

is my friend Johnson. I was just telling him about your world-famous pasta."

"You are too kind..." He hesitated, then went on: "Although you ought to tell that to Alfonzo. He will be most pleased to hear it."

"Speaking of Alfonzo, is he here, by any chance?" Maya asked.

"He is in the kitchen... but he is, ah, busy at the moment. I will send him up to see you later. Let me find you a table first."

He beckoned them to follow, leading them to a table at the far end of the garden shaded by the long, leafy vines of the willow tree. There was a small, flickering torch on one side that smelled of burnt citrus.

"The best seat in the house for you, my dear," said Miguel as he laid a napkin on her lap before darting off to see another customer.

Maya gazed around the garden. "It's great here, isn't it, Johnson?"

Johnson could hear insects buzzing and singing with the excitement of dusk, and the odd bird chirping in delight. It was magical. He glanced at Maya, then back to the surrounding garden.

Maya waited for him to respond. "Are you okay?" she asked.

Johnson nodded. "I don't know," he said after a time, then added quietly, "It's just nice to be out doing things... with you. I feel like I haven't been out enough of late. I mean, this is the first time I've been anywhere like this for ages. It's like I've missed so much by staying at my home in the Village."

Maya toyed with her hair. "True. But there's no point living in the past, Johnson. It's gone and not coming back."

"I guess," he replied.

4.

"This is the present," Maya said, her eyes wide and full of life. "Right now! The only time I ever live, have ever lived, is right now. There is nothing else. It is now. So forget what has been, and be as you want to be."

Johnson felt a quiver of excitement. "Yeah, that makes sense,' he said. "Live for now. This moment." He smiled. "And who knows about the future? You or I could be blown up at any moment by a stray bomb from an anti-globalist."

"You mean a wasp or some murderous fucking police drone," she replied, spitting anger with her words. She sat stone-faced for a moment, then took a deep breath, composed herself and went on: "And that would be it. So, we have to live for the now. Not for yesterday or tomorrow, but for today, for this moment right now." She leaned across the table and put her hand on his. She rubbed his hand gently.

Johnson nodded. "But we still need to have enough for tomorrow."

"What is enough, Johnson?

"I don't know... enough food and water, a place to live," he replied. "Access to the internet, I guess, and an Eye-Tab."

"Yeah, you need those things. All except an Eye-Tab," she giggled. "And maybe you need them less than you think, or less often at least. There are ways to get hold of those necessities that are easier, or better for the soul, than the way people get them now." She seemed to get agitated with her own words. "You don't need to work at a big company all your life just so you can stay in their employee housing and have a place to sleep between constant days of work."

"We all do that," Johnson mumbled.

She ignored him. "Right now, we should be drinking wine. For that is living in the moment. And look, Miguel is here, right on... *time.*" She winked, then gestured to the waiter, who had returned to their table. "Miguel, my dear friend," she smiled and put her hands together over her heart, "can you get us some wine, please?"

"Of course!" He poured them both water and then put the clear glass bottle on the table next to the vase. "What wine would you like? Red or white?"

"Most definitely red," Maya replied. She turned to Johnson. "Is that okay for you?"

He shrugged. He hadn't drunk much wine. It was a luxury. It didn't grow well in the Trade Bloc. Something to do with changes in temperatures and weather patterns meant the vineyards couldn't get enough water and the soil had altered, leaching a compound that had ruined years of grape growing tradition.

"Are you sure? I could drink beer," he spluttered, wondering if he might not be able to afford the wine.

"It's fine," said Maya, "Miguel will look after us." She touched his arm again. "They have great wine here. They get it specially delivered from the Eurozone."

Johnson's mouth hung open slightly, as he wondered how they got the wine through Customs, given the NABOJ Trade Bloc was in a trade war with the Eurozone, which had recently been escalated by Chief Officer Hope's ongoing war of words with the European CEO.

"Alfonzo!" shouted Maya, as the chef appeared at their table, his white chef's hat flopping forward over his eyes. She jumped up and hugged him, squeezing her tiny frame into the man's big belly. She whispered something quietly in his ear. He nodded and gave her a kiss on the cheek. He put a thick hairy arm around her waist.

"This is Johnson," she said.

He put his hand out and Johnson shook it. "I'm Alfonzo," he said. "You work at Gorilla Industries, right?"

"That's right!" said Johnson, wondering how he knew.

"This girl here," Alfonzo looked at Maya, "is an amazing girl. You are a lucky man, Johnson."

Maya laughed. "Stop it, Alfonzo."

"I am serious. She has saved my life many times."

"The restaurant is looking great," Maya said.

"Except for the customers," Alfonzo replied. "It's Saturday night, which should be the busiest night of the week, and we have only a few people here." He pointed around the restaurant. Inside, there was a grey-haired elderly couple seated silently by a window, and behind them a large family split across two tables. The garden was empty, apart from two other young couples and a bearded man dressed in a black shirt and pants and wearing a beret. He sat alone, drinking wine while scribbling furiously in a book.

"It's still early," Johnson said diplomatically. "A lot of people don't finish work till now."

"That's very true, sir. It will be fine. We have our ways and means." He shrugged his shoulders. "Not having customers can have its benefits," he added with a laugh. "Now what can I get you tonight? Remember, everything is on the house."

Johnson smiled, relieved about the cost of the wine, but twinged with guilt, given there were so few customers. "I'm happy to pay," he offered.

"Nonsense... our Maya never pays. Not here. Not if I have anything to do with it."

"Thank you, Alfonzo, that's very kind of you." She gave him

another hug, and then sat down in her chair. "You always make such wonderful pasta, so two bowls of whatever you think we ought to try."

"That will be my pleasure. I know just the thing."

"Miguel was going to get us some wine as well."

"I'll send him out. I'd better get back to the kitchen so I can make you this pasta *especial*... you will love it," Alfonzo said with a wink. "It is great to see you, as always... ah, Maya." He squeezed her shoulder. "Good to meet you too, Master Johnson." He gave Johnson a long, gazing look, and then turned back to the kitchen. "We will talk later," he said, over his shoulder, as he walked away.

"Sure," Maya said to the disappearing figure. She turned back to Johnson. "He's a wonderful man, our Alfonzo."

"How do you know him?"

She paused. "From around, you know," she said, avoiding Johnson's gaze.

"Was he your boyfriend?" he asked nervously.

Maya laughed. "What? Alfonzo? Not likely. We did keep each other company once or twice, but that was a long time ago now."

"So that's how you met?"

She laughed again and shuffled in her seat. "How about you, Johnson, have you had any girlfriends before?"

He looked into her eyes – her pupils widened. She was gazing back at him with an insatiable appetite for his words. He felt more confident. "There was a girl called Rachael, back in school," he began.

"Ah, school crushes are my favourite. What happened? Tell me everything."

Johnson told Maya the story of the real Rachael: his love for her for all those years, and then their moment of passion on the school oval. How they had seen each other for a few months after, spending time in his bedroom listening to music, and at the beach, where they made up words with new meanings created from nothing – 'Champabulous' had been his favourite. He had fallen deeply in love with her. And then she left the school and never came back. Then their online communication had drifted, until she eventually stopped responding, leaving him shattered, a broken teenager with a whole life still ahead of him. He had only ever told Eileen from work about it, and of course Conrad knew – he had lived through the pain with Johnson, or at least heard about it every day for months and months on end. As he told Maya, he felt a warm glow in the quiet relief of finally letting go of something he should have let go of a long time ago.

Miguel brought the bread and wine. He poured two glasses to the top. "This here is a Syrah," he said, pointing at the bottle, which didn't have a label. "You will like it, I promise."

They thanked Miguel and he left them to their wine.

"What shall we toast to?" Maya asked.

"I don't know," Johnson replied.

"What about to us," she suggested seductively.

They clinked glasses.

He took a long sip of the wine. It tasted like velvet in his mouth, then sour as he swallowed it down, but with a hint of dark chocolate. He relaxed and took another sip. "To us," he said, raising his glass again.

They ate their meal, talking throughout, telling stories of their lives. Maya had done so much. She had seen parts of the world that Johnson had only read and dreamt about. He wondered how she had fitted it all in. She seemed so young and carefree yet experienced beyond her years.

"Where did you work before Gorilla Industries?" he asked as their conversation wound its way back to what had brought them together.

"Lots of places, but none for long. Before that, I studied at university."

"The School of Economics?"

"No. It was a real university. I studied arts and philosophy. It was a creative university. An institute for learning. Plato would have been proud."

"Where was that?" he asked. He wanted to ask who Plato was too, but let it slide.

"It doesn't exist now. They shut it down... like most good universities. Nearly everyone has to study Economics or go to one of the private business schools if they want to do further study. It's all part of their plan. They don't want a smart society - educated people would demand better. And if everyone who goes to university studies business, as taught by them, and learns to love capital, then the whole system keeps rolling on. Education now, like everything, is about money, and making more money and committing people to the ideals of money."

Johnson listened, unsure how to respond. He was saved by Miguel, who brought out their pasta in white bowls and placed a tray of condiments on the table by the flowers. Johnson watched as Maya covered her pasta with parmesan cheese and added some chilli oil. Johnson followed suit. He had never tasted anything as delicious, especially not in all his years eating synthetic food at the Gorilla Industries employee café.

5.

As Johnson returned from the toilet, his belly full of pasta and ice cream and wine, he saw Maya's chair was empty. *She must be in the bathroom,* he thought. He sat down and waited, fiddling with the bowl of parmesan cheese still on the table in front of him.

He stood up and paced the garden, which was now half-filled with customers. Some looked at him oddly as he walked between their tables, as if he were another lost soul unable to be helped. He went over to the garden and looked at the flowering shrubs. He picked a small white flower that had only just bloomed, thinking he might give it to Maya. He examined the delicate petals, trying to marvel at their perfect symmetry, but couldn't stop the typhoon of anxious thoughts swirling in his mind.

After 20 minutes, Johnson was so concerned that he rushed maniacally inside the restaurant, his eyes darting about in a desperate bid to find her.

Miguel was at the bar, mixing a drink.

Johnson marched up to the bar. "Hi Miguel," he said.

Miguel looked up from his drink.

"Do you know where Maya went?" Johnson asked, trying to keep calm.

"Hold on a minute." Miguel walked down a set of stairs behind the bar. Johnson heard a knock and then a door open. He could hear Miguel talking, and then, to his relief, he heard *her* voice.

Miguel reappeared at the top of the stairs. "She is coming."

A moment later, Maya walked up, followed by Alfonzo.

She walked over and grabbed Johnson around the waist. She kissed him on the cheek, then whispered in his ear: "Let's go somewhere more private."

Johnson didn't know what to say. He thanked Miguel and Alfonzo for the meal with exaggerated effect, covering up the wave of embarrassment that had hit him.

"See you soon," Alfonzo said. "Take care of her," he told Johnson as they shook hands. "Not that she needs taking care of," he winked.

"Bye Alfonzo," Maya said with a wave. They walked out, arm in arm.

"Where did you want to go?" Johnson asked as they strolled down the street.

"I know a guesthouse, not far from here, where we can go, where I can have *you*." She looked at Johnson then kissed him on the mouth. He kissed back, softly at first then more passionately. He was aroused and kept kissing. "Let's go," he said.

She took him to an old, dilapidated hotel around the corner. It wasn't far from the restaurant, but here everything seemed faded and crumbly, as if they had passed over the last line of care and concern.

Maya went in first and talked to the lady at reception. There was a glass front between them. Johnson peered inside, surprised to see a real person behind the desk and not a machine. Maya leaned in and whispered to the lady. The lady looked spaced out, as if she wasn't really there. But after a brief pause, she put a key in a sliding drawer under the glass and shunted it forward.

"Come on," Maya shouted as she raced up the cracked staircase.

5.

He followed her carelessly up the stairs to the room. He watched as she unlocked the door. Johnson had never seen a metal key before. He had only ever used swipe cards or electronic click-buttons.

The room was dark and dusty. There was nothing in it, save for the double bed in the middle, a small desk, and an old television on a cabinet in the corner. The television looked like a relic from a different age. A mouldy rug covered half the wooden floor.

Maya kissed Johnson and dragged him over to the bed. They flopped down together. He kissed her deeply, his tongue filling her mouth. She tasted like basil and tomato from the pasta sauce. He put his hands on her breasts and felt her bra. She tore off his shirt and he pulled hers up as far as it would go. He was desperate to see her naked body, but also incredibly nervous about the situation.

He ripped at her bra but couldn't undo it. She unclasped it for him. He dived in, kissing her nipples. He grabbed hold of her breasts awkwardly. He wanted to suck them – honey-brown skin with a dark nipple. He kissed her nipples over and over, then undid her white pants and pulled them down past her thighs. He got up and took his pants off. She giggled as he ripped off her underpants. He was hard. He wanted her.

She held him against her. She grabbed his penis and played around, pushing it against her pubic mound. She was wet and ready. He slid inside her. She gasped. "I want you," she said. "I want you too," he said as he moved inside her – fast at first, then slower as he found her rhythm. She moved down against him, so he was higher and deeper. Suddenly, he couldn't contain himself any longer. He tried to stop, but it was too late. He slowed and then went on for a bit, hoping she hadn't noticed.

She looked into his eyes. "Did you finish?"

He nodded, slightly ashamed. He rolled over onto his side.

"It's okay," she said. "It was nice to have you inside me. We will just have to go again." She touched him. He was slowly softening. "When you are ready. When this is ready again..." She laughed as she rubbed him gently with her hands.

He felt relieved. Even in this moment of shame, he still felt good to be here with her. She held him tightly. He kissed her again. He hadn't done it with a real woman for so long, he had forgotten what it felt like. The wetness, the warmth, the closeness of touch, of her skin on his, the feeling of actually being inside her – it could never be replaced by virtual sex. No matter the impossible beauty of the virtual girl he had designed, she could never be real, and she could never make him feel alive.

He knew he would be hard again soon. Maya was too beautiful – her skin so soft, her eyes so enticing, with lips he wanted desperately to kiss. Her voice was magnetic, attracting him, wanting him, inspiring him to be more than he was. He wanted her. He wanted to be inside her again. He wanted to never leave this room.

6.

As quietly as possible, Una pulled a Portable Internet Device from her bag. It was all she had in there beyond the anonymous chip card and a make-up kit. It was better to have nothing, to be no one.

She opened the dark web porthole, knowing it was safe to do so from here, and found the secure messaging application she always used. She logged into her fake account – set up before the mission for a moment like this when she couldn't help herself. She was not allowed to communicate with any of them. Not while things were in motion. It was too risky, could jeopardise everything... but she had her weaknesses too. And this was their little secret, like two sisters hiding their silly made-up games from mum and dad.

She scrolled through to the contact Parks had given her. It was another alias account, made from stolen information. Really, they were stolen identities, secure for them, but also creating plausible deniability for those whose identities they used – without consent, without a trace. That's what they hoped anyway.

There was nothing from Parks.

Una began to type out the words she always used for her friend – the words which somehow said all was okay and things were running smoothly. There would likely come a time when it would no longer be possible – when one or both had been arrested or taken out by wasps, which was probably preferable. But for now, it made her feel good, still connected to the people she loved.

They were humanists after all. Fighting for a better world, she may never see or know. But there was always hope. And that's why she did what she had too... and that was always the catch. There were so many moments when she worried that maybe she'd gone too far, compromised another soul for their ends. *Was this another one?* she wondered, as she looked sadly at the Information Editor by her side, knowing the answer she didn't really want to know.

She buried the thought, looked over her message: *The seeds are sewn, ready to flower, and when they do, we will have sunshine again.* She added two kisses and a heart icon, and then sent the message with a tap. She grabbed a cleansing wipe from the make-up kit, wiped the screen clean, then gently snapped the PID case shut and lay back down on her side of the bed.

7.

He woke up and saw her lying naked beside him. He ran his hand across her thighs and traced her smooth, soft skin up to her belly button. He stroked under her navel for a few moments. He felt a sudden and urgent attraction to this part of her body and couldn't leave it alone. He gently rubbed under her belly then moved up to her breasts. She awoke and they made love once more.

"Last night was the best night of my life," he said, panting heavily.

She smiled and kissed him again. "You are a beautiful soul, but... oh so innocent." She got up and went to the bathroom.

He heard the water running. He lay back, gleaming. He listened to the sounds of her showering, not really believing his luck. It was as if the rest of his life had been a prelude to this moment, a dress rehearsal for the real thing.

"Now, what are we going to do today?" she asked as she came back from the bathroom, a towel around her waist, water dripping from her thick brown hair onto her neck and breasts. He wanted to lick off the droplets as they slid down her body like skiers on a chute. He wanted to make love to her again.

"I'm not sure. I guess I need to get back to the Gorilla Compound," Johnson replied. "I should probably go to the School of Economics at some point this morning too," he added.

"What, for a sermon?"

He nodded.

"Economics sermons are ridiculous," she snapped.

"Shhhh," whispered Johnson. The authorities would not take kindly to them bad mouthing the one community event that was supported by all – the employees, the Government, the private companies, the elites, and the all-powerful corporations.

"Don't worry," she said as she dropped her towel and sat on the side of the bed. "This place is fine. There are no bugs here."

"That's cool." He sat up on the bed. "I'd better get up and have a shower."

She put on her knickers and white three-quarter pants from yesterday. "Why would you want to go to the School of Economics anyway? It's a complete waste of time."

"Do you mean that?"

"Yes, of course. Praying for the Economy to be strong – how silly! We don't need growth. We need to stop growth."

"Growth is good, right? It keeps people employed, and in jobs."

"Yes, and our world is screwed as a result. You cannot have infinite growth in a finite world. Something has to give. Look at global warming and rising sea levels and pollution and the extinction of animals." She paused and took a breath. "And the chopping down of forests... pollution in the oceans and waterways, the destruction of nature, and farmlands that have been turned into dustbowls. You think these are not the result of the continued drive for growth and profit. Eventually everything is used up and spat out... and then there is nothing left."

She put on her black shirt and buttoned it up. She turned to Johnson, her eyes trained onto his, her shoulders slumped forward, and said, "You don't think humans have got long left to live, do you?"

7.

He slowly got off the bed. "Look, you don't have to convince me," he said defensively. "I know how much humans have destroyed the planet, and I know what can happen with mining and chemicals." He thought of his mother and stopped, unable to speak for a moment, his eyes welling up as he remembered what she had been through.

"I'm glad you agree," Maya replied, "because it all has to stop, the whole damn machine, otherwise we are all doomed... if this is not doomed already."

There was a pause in their talk, as Johnson excused himself and went for a long shower.

When he returned, Maya was dressed with her handbag hanging over one shoulder. She stood with her hands on her hips, seemingly ready for anything. "Let's go to the Botanical Gardens and see all the trees and plants they have there. We can get back to nature; enjoy what's left." She smiled.

Johnson couldn't resist her. He walked over and pulled Maya in towards him.

"Oh, and what about the Millennium Museum?" she said excitedly. "That would be great. We could see all the incredible things they had at the turn of the century," Maya said between kisses.

"Yeah, whatever you think," he replied, not caring what they did, as long as it was with her.

"We can do both," she declared. "Now get dressed so we can get on with the day. There is so much to see. I can't wait to smell the flowers."

At the entry to the Botanical Gardens was a statue of the bearded 114-year-old philanthropist and options trillionaire Amos

Harralampedes, who'd donated the gardens to the people some years earlier. They walked between two rows of palm trees and reached a crossroads with signs to various sections of the park.

She took his hand and led him down the path on the left. They arrived at the enclosed tropical section. She took him on a guided tour, telling him about jungles in parts of the world that he scarcely knew existed, and of great forests that had been chopped down to grow crops and grains. "They lopped so many trees in the Latin Territories and parts of South-East Asia to force open new space to grow palm oil, or grain for farm animals, to meet the needs of a growing world population," she said seriously, "that eventually the earth choked up, unable to breathe."

"That's why cattle farming got banned, right?" he said.

"Humans are reactive creatures," Maya explained as they walked beneath a row of high palms and along a path that swept between ferns and other plants that Johnson had never seen before. They had wide vibrant green leaves and stocky brown trunks, looking like oversized bonsais – shrunk down and then blown back up and left all out of proportion.

She went on: "It was only when things got really bad that anyone did anything about it. When the elites who run the world started to worry for themselves and their families... that's when they took action and banned cattle farming. They don't care about the rest of us. We are an inconvenience." She stopped on the track. "You can bet there are a few farms out there, hidden away from prying eyes, with paddocks filled with cows, making sure the elites still get enough beef to placate their fat, greedy stomachs."

Johnson felt the sting in Maya's voice. He stopped a few yards ahead, thinking. He had never been very political and rarely spoke about such things to anyone. He avoided it for his own safety and sanity. Plus, it was not really acceptable for an Information Editor at Gorilla Industries, where reactionary thought was cut off before it could infect the network, like a gangrenous leg severed to save the rest of the body. He walked on; glad they were surrounded by trees and not security wasps.

"What about genetically created beef?" he asked, breaking the silence, thinking about his own experiences eating Beef-o. "You know the stuff they make in the labs."

"I don't know what natural laws are being broken in those places, and what freaky Dr Moreau creations they are making in secret, but at least it's not destroying us," she replied, as they marched on, reaching a fork in the road. "Come, let me show you my favourite garden," she said, skipping off down a path to the left.

After a short walk, they reached two gardens separated by a tiled walkway.

"This is the cactus garden," Maya announced.

There were tall cacti that reached for the heavens, some sprouting from the earth like rockets shooting for the Coca-Cola moon, and others that looked like spiky pitch forks - able to ward off hungry mammals but futile against moths and caterpillars. Some were almost spongy, with dull leaves that wouldn't look out of place on an asteroid or among the coral in the shallows of an atoll.

Johnson walked around in a trance-like state. He had never seen such plants. He was an alien turning up on a new planet and seeing everything for the first time. Maya told him that many of the plants grew in the Latin Territories, in the desert areas of the north, which had been increasing with each passing year - forcing more and more migrants north and south in search of food and water.

"Is that where you are from," Johnson asked as they sat on a wall, "the Latin Territories?"

"Originally, yes," she replied. "We came by boat."

Johnson was quiet for a moment. He remembered the fallout from the boat people saga when migrants streamed across the seas in an attempt to outrun the devastation of climate change. They had been turned back in droves, many even killed. "How was that?" he asked a little nervously.

"I was a baby. My father didn't make it."

Maya didn't seem to want to explain further, and Johnson decided not to push it – not quite sure whether that meant he hadn't made the journey at all, or that he had died there out at sea, crammed into a boat like so many others.

"And what about your father, is he still around?" Maya asked, her demeanour changing with the question.

"Yeah, well sort of. He's alive but not around."

"What do you mean by that?" asked Maya.

Johnson took a deep breath, and then said: "He wasn't the same after Mum's death. He didn't last long at work after that. He couldn't maintain his position and lost the plot a bit. I tried to help but couldn't because of my job, so I had to put him in a home."

"A private home?"

"No. He didn't have any money because he'd spent it all on Mum's treatment, and About-Face wouldn't give him a company pension because of the merger and the way things ended there... so he had to go into a Government retirement home in the end." Johnson looked out across the gardens. "At least he has a place to stay."

Maya fell silent.

"He'd sold the family home to pay her hospital fees, and then when he got sacked, there was no place to go. He stayed with me briefly, in the Gorilla Compound, but he couldn't stay long. They wouldn't let him. That's when I took him to the home. And now they won't let me see him. It's part of the rules. Once they go in... that's it, you can't see them again."

"I know about the homes," Maya said, biting at her lip. She looked away, towards the fountain, and wiped her cheek, then muttered something under her breath.

Johnson put his hand on Maya's knee and gently squeezed, hoping to make her feel better, but she jumped up, clearly agitated.

They left the cactus garden behind with their pained conversation, and circled around the rest of the Botanical Gardens, looking first at the rose garden and then the palm trees.

'Let's have a picnic,' suggested Maya suddenly.

Johnson held out his arms and took in the sun's rays of life-affirming light, and then bounced down the path, grabbing Maya's hands and twirling her around him in one big arc. He couldn't remember the last time he had danced like this, and he felt liberated and free in the beauty of his surroundings.

Johnson stopped at a kiosk and bought some pre-made lunch rolls and a cake to share. They sat in a shady spot under a tree, avoiding the intensity of the sun. It was a hot day for this time of year, but the weather was often extreme, ranging from super-hot to super-cold, with weeks of torrential rain and then months of drought – the results of 50 years of severe climate change. If he believed Conrad, then it was all a hoax created by ecowarriors and solar companies – for what purpose, he never knew, and Conrad had never properly explained.

But, right now, Johnson didn't care. He rolled over and gave

Maya a long heavy kiss. He wanted to keep kissing her and then to make love right there on the grass, but he could see other people walking around. He didn't want to cause a scene. He hadn't heard or seen any wasps whilst in the gardens, but they would be around, waiting to pounce. The private security forces were always looking for more people to arrest, to fill up the jails that the private prison companies – Incarcer8 Ltd and Globohold – had built in every city and trade bloc state.

8.

The Millennium Museum was in an old sandstone building not far from the car-grid. They walked inside through the glass entry doors and down a long hallway, and then turned onto a ramp that led to the second level.

Maya paid the entry fee and the two went through the ticket gate, along a carpeted area, and into a large room where everything was painted black. Along the edge, spaced equally apart, were glass cabinets displaying items of historical significance.

Johnson walked up to the first display. It had a red telephone with a twirled-up chord and a handset on one side. He read the description on the wall:

The telephone was invented by Alexander Graham Bell in 1875. It allowed two people to speak over a great distance through a device designed for sound waves to be converted into electrical energy, transmitted down a wire and heard at a receiver, where it was converted back into sound. It was used extensively throughout the 20th century until it was replaced by the mobile phone, which transmits sound through radio waves. The mobile phone is still used today, but verbal communication has been commonly replaced by email and other message-based services that allow communication without a direct, real-time link.

Maya was standing at a case with a typewriter inside. Johnson trotted over and peered in at the typewriter. He'd seen pictures of typewriters in books. People barely typed these days, as most written documents used voice-to-text applications. Typing had become another unnecessary skill, lost to humanity like map-reading or mathematics.

They moved on and walked inside a small, dark room off to the side. It was spherical with four long glass cabinets arranged in a semi-circle. He went up to the first cabinet and peered at the display. There was a miniature mine with 'COAL' written across the wooden-beam entrance. Next to it was a model of a steam engine with a railroad running up to a factory, which had a boiler and two fat chimneys pumping replica smoke into the air.

There was a red button on the front of the cabinet. Johnson pressed it and heard a computerised voice say: "*The big economic shifts in history have one thing in common: breakthroughs in energy, communications and transport technology at around the same time. During the First Industrial Revolution in 19th-century Britain, advances in steam technology led to the development of the steam-powered printing press and the steam locomotive, which, in turn, led to the creation of the mass media and the railways. These breakthroughs were also underpinned by a new energy source in cheap coal.*"

Johnson walked around to the next diorama. It was a model of a petrol station with three extravagant cars painted in bright colours, with elegant lines and shiny wheels.

"I can't believe everyone used to drive around in cars," he said.

"It was a different time," Maya answered.

"Lots of people died on the roads because people didn't know how to drive properly," he added.

"At least they could go where they wanted," she shot back.

"What do you mean?" Johnson asked slowly. "We can go where we want, can't we?"

"Where the car-grid goes, more like it, and that's only if it wants to take you there. Remember, you can always be blacklisted, Johnson, and then you may not be able to go anywhere."

He walked to the third glass cabinet. Inside was a cluster of houses with solar panels on the roofs. Some of the houses were open. They each had a person sitting inside at a desk, using a computer. He pressed the button underneath and the autorrator started up again: *"An even more seismic revolution occurred during this century. The convergence of renewable – especially solar – energy, the communications internet and self-driving electric vehicles gave rise to a technology platform called the Internet of Things: the embedding of computing devices into everyday objects, which send and receive data through the internet. Over 500 billion devices currently link farms, mines, the electricity grid, the car-grid, production lines, transport networks, warehouses and recycling systems to the internet."*

He turned to Maya. "This is amazing," he said.

"Yeah. It's interesting stuff, isn't it? The way the world changed so rapidly only a few decades ago. The question is: did it change for the better?"

He stood quietly, watching her wide eyes. Not quite sure how to respond.

"And that was before they regulated the internet."

They moved along to the final cabinet. There was a house with a robot inside working at a computer. Beyond it was a model of the solar system with rays of light flying in all directions. *"We are on the cusp of a new revolution in the creation of full artificial intelligence. How it will change the world is not yet known. But the next revolution could have an untold impact on daily life. With artificial intelligence, it is possible that human beings could make systems with infinite knowledge and intelligence, giving them the power and knowledge of gods."*

Johnson stood, looking at the robot and the solar system, wondering for a moment what the future held. He looked at Maya. She sighed.

They walked back out into the main room and checked out the other displays.

The next room was lighter, with wooden floors. It was filled with colourful displays that were attached to the walls and floor like sculptures in an art gallery. Johnson's favourite was the *World Money* exhibit. It had a map of the old world, pre-trade blocs, with hundreds of countries and flags. Next to each country was a banknote – something that seemed so odd to him now.

"People must have been robbed all the time," he said with a laugh.

"Yeah, but they were free." She held up her arm and pointed to her wrist, where there was a red mark running down. And can you be truly free with one of these?"

Johnson looked forebodingly down at his own wrist chip. There was no mark, just a little raise in the skin where the chip had been inserted. It certainly made transactions easy, efficiency perhaps at the expense of control. And he wondered, for a moment, what else they could be used for?

They left the museum, hand in hand once more, a slight despondency hanging over Johson as they walked slowly across the road.

8.

As the light began to fade, Maya turned to him. "I'd better get going," she said.

"Do you have to?" he asked.

"Yes. And so do you."

"I guess, but I don't want to."

"That's a lovely thing to say, Johnson." She leaned in and kissed him, then gave him a long hug.

"Where can I find you?" he asked.

"At Gorilla Industries, of course," she answered, grinning.

"Why don't we share a car back there together," he suggested hopefully.

"You know I can't," she replied without further enlightenment. "And besides, I have to go back and see someone about..." she trailed off, and instead squeezed his hand.

Johnson felt a twinge of jealousy, wondering if the 'someone' she had to see may be Alfonzo. "Do you have a work email I can contact you on?" he asked as he rubbed at his arm. "Or an AppChat handle?"

"I don't have any of those," she giggled.

"About-Face?" asked Johnson.

"I hate all those social media pages."

"Me too," he replied not-entirely-honestly.

She drew him before her, taking him by both hands. "I work in your building, on the 112th floor. I will see you at the cafeteria, tomorrow or the next day... I'll come and find you. Don't worry about it, Johnson. This is a good thing. I'm not going to let it slip away."

Johnson felt relieved. He pulled her close and kissed her deeply on the mouth. She unclasped herself from his grip.

"Why don't you put your contact details in my PID," she said as she pulled a Portable Internet Device from her handbag. She held it up, taking a picture of them together, then one just of him, of his face alone silhouetted against the cityscape, before handing the PID over to his outstretched palm.

"What details do you want?" he asked.

"Put in whatever, everything... your email address and AppChat handle, if you have one. Save it under 'Johnson'. And put in your work email too. Even your login details," she added with a laugh. "That's probably the easiest way for me to contact you."

He eagerly filled out his details, his thumbs tapping gently on the PID's in-built digital keypad, and then handed it back.

She snapped the case shut and carefully placed it in her bag.

Johnson nuzzled in beside her, his arms around her waist. He didn't want to let go.

"Now, I really must be going," she said, pulling herself away from his outstretched hands. As he let her go, she suddenly stopped and turned back to him. "You are a good man, Johnson," she said, her voice crackling slightly. "Too good for Gorilla Industries. Don't let them beat you down."

9.

He runs his hand through a clump of brown grass. It is soft to touch, softer than he'd expected. The land is parched, and rocks are visible among the dry vegetation. He is pushed from behind and nearly falls into a bracken-filled ditch at the side of the path. He regains his balance just in time, his feet saving the day with unusual grace. He turns around and looks angrily at his brother. His brother has a smile wrapped across his face; the same mischievous smile Johnson has seen a thousand times.

"Fuck off, Goliath," he says.

"Don't swear!" barks his mother, who is walking up ahead.

He thinks of telling her that he was pushed, explaining himself, but doesn't bother. He glares at his brother, then trots up beside his mother. On her left is her sister, his aunt. They are talking, reminiscing about their life together as children growing up on the farm that his auntie now runs.

"This paddock was filled with sheep," his mother says.

"Yeah, there were thousands," replies his aunt.

"There is nothing like the sight of a mob of sheep running together in unison, sheep dogs herding them through the scrub."

He grunts approvingly, imagining their white woolly backs covering the hillside.

"I'd love to have more sheep, but there's not enough grass to feed them," his auntie adds. "It doesn't grow well enough nowadays."

"It's a shame," says his mother.

Johnson picks up a long stick. It has fallen from a dying tree a few yards off the track. He walks with it, pushing it into the ground like it's a walking stick. Goliath grabs him from behind, pulling his arms tightly into his chest, holding him there for a second, then runs off ahead.

He wishes his dad was here. A holiday with the whole family would have been nice, but he couldn't come. As always, he had to work; was busy with the company and couldn't afford to take the time off... which left Johnson, Goliath, and their mother, to come up in the car without him.

Suddenly, the ground shakes. It reverberates around the surrounding hillside like an echo. For a moment, it feels like they're on a roller-coaster.

"Earthquake!" shouts his auntie.

Johnson drops to the ground in fear. Everyone else stands still, waiting for God's wrath to pass over them, or at least until the last tremor dissipates. It is like a long note at the climax of a symphony; it holds in the air for what seems like an eternity, and as the earth settles, he's not quite sure if it is still moving, vibrating ever so slightly, or has reached its final peace.

"Blame the gas fracking," his mother proclaims. "It's been going on since we were kids. They've destroyed this place."

"Is that why it looks like the surface of the moon?" Johnson asks, thinking of an article he read about a second moon they want to put up in the sky as a tribute to human ingenuity.

"Hear that, Sis, your nephew thinks it looks like the moon around here."

"He's not wrong," replies his aunt. "But it's not the only land that's been ruined for mining and gas operations." She bends down and grabs a handful of soil. She releases it slowly, the grains falling at an angle in the wind.

His mother nods in agreement.

"It's not the worst of it, either," says his auntie sternly. "They said it was harmless too, the bastards... Ha! Harmless! The water supplies are ruined. The underground aquifers are filled with noxious chemicals."

He walks up to his aunt and puts his arm around her. She gently rubs the back of his green puffy jacket. Up ahead, his brother stops and turns around. "You coming?" he shouts.

"Just a minute, honey," his mum replies. She stands next to them, her sister still squatting in a patch of red-brown earth. "We can't drink the water, can we?" his mum asks while shielding the sun from her eyes, her other hand resting on her hip.

"Not really," answers his aunt. "It's dangerous. There are thousands of chemicals in here – in the water table, in this soil – which are carcinogenic. They were used to release the gas held inside the rocks, and they are giving cancer to the people in this town."

His mother looks horrified. "We are drinking rainwater, right?" she asks, rubbing nervously at her arm.

"Hurry up," calls Goliath.

"We are coming," she replies, not looking away from her sister.

"Yeaahh, now we are, and thankfully we have some drums of water, in case we run low. But when you and I grew up here... we drank the water."

"That was before the issues, though," his mum says.

"There were chemicals in the water even back then," his aunt replies. "They have been fracking for a long time, remember, since we were little kids."

His mother's face drops, and she places her hand on her chest as if she is about to be sick. She catches herself and stands up quickly, covering her moment of weakness with an awkward smile.

"Is everything okay, Mum?" Johnson asks.

"Yes, dear, it's fine," she says while looking away, as if she doesn't want to tell him everything. He sees a tear in her eye, and watches as she clutches at her chest again.

His auntie looks at his mother accusingly. She starts to speak but is cut off.

"I've just got some pain under my ribs, is all," says his mum. "I must have slept badly in that old bed of mine," she laughs.

She runs after Goliath, grabbing him in a bear hug. He squirms his way out. She relents, and instead rests her slender arm on his broadening shoulders. They walk off into the distance together - mother and eldest son.

10.

A message popped up on Johnson's AppChat: *You want to watch the grand final tonight?*

It was the third message this week from Conrad about the game. Johnson didn't respond. A few moments later another message arrived: *Come-on Jay, the final. Zucks v Globals.*

Johnson knew how much his continued silence would be annoying his football-obsessed friend. The Chargers weren't playing but Conrad liked to watch every match he could, even those played in the Eurozone or the Re-formed Soviet Union, and this was the Four Pillars Cup Final. Johnson was glad Amazon-Phizo had been knocked out by the IBC Globals in the preliminary final, and he always liked to see the About-Face Zucks get beaten, but he hadn't been thinking much about football. His mind was elsewhere.

He held off responding to Conrad for as long as possible, hoping desperately for the long-awaited message from Maya, and a repeat of last weekend's activities, but the final started in less than an hour, and even he had to admit a temporary defeat.

Sorry for the delay getting back to you, Conrad, been busy at work. I'm up for the final, amigo, but I'll be late.

Are you working now? What time do you finish? appeared quickly on the instant messenger.

17:00, unfortunately.

The game started slightly earlier than normal on Grand Final Saturday – in one of the few remaining traditions from the days when the clubs represented the cities, and not companies. It meant he would miss the first half, and all the pre-game entertainment, which was usually a bit of a spectacle.

Don't they give you Grand Final Saturday off?

Not at Gorilla Industries, sadly.

Can't you get out earlier?

Kidding, right? Only a death in the family or a special sermon at the School of Economics is grounds for getting out early.

Johnson didn't want to work. He was unmotivated, tired, and slightly pained by Maya's continued absence. He wasn't in the mood to finish his allotted tasks. *I could always do it tomorrow,* he considered. It wasn't allowed, but then nothing was *allowed*.

Normally, he'd send an email back to the Information Manager with a final summary of the newspapers, blogs, vlogs and opinion pieces he'd gone through during the workday, marked up with any edits he'd made, along with all the drafts and final versions of any newly created 'paid' content. *Not today!* He was tired of doing the same tasks day in, day out. He only had one life, and he felt as if he was wasting it, one edit at a time. He spent so much time at Gorilla Industries – stuck in the stuffy office, staring at a screen – and he was hardly appreciated by his employer. He'd never received a commendation, at least not since those few 'employee of the month' awards in his early years. No bonuses for all his hard work; and he'd only received three small pay rises in nearly nine years, which were all tied to inflation.

"Fuck them all," he said to himself as he made the rapid decision to walk right out of there and go home. He was about to log off his computer, but then thought better of it and left it running. That way, if they traced his work log, it would appear as though he'd continued working right through to the end of the day.

He looked around the office. Everyone else on his floor was working furiously, their heads down, concentrating on whatever task they had been assigned by their respective managers. No one even noticed him leave. The Information Manager would not receive Johnson's daily report, but he could always send it off tomorrow and blame a computer glitch or the server. He was going to go and have a drink and watch the game with Conrad live on his holo-vision. *Forget Maya,* he thought, *she will contact me when she's ready.*

He flicked on his Eye-Tab and sent a message to Conrad: *Just left. Heading home now.*

Nice. See you on the big screen.

He headed down in the lift. He was excited but also a little apprehensive, knowing he was about to be in breach of the employee code of conduct. He felt a wave of courage surge through him as he left the tower behind him.

He looked around the courtyard, hoping not to bump into Melville or any employees he knew... apart from Maya. He hoped to see her at every turn and had done all week.

She wasn't there. Nobody was. The yard area was completely empty.

As he walked across at a rapid pace, he thought he heard a low pounding, as if a bass drum were beating up at the ground from beneath its surface. He stopped and looked around, not knowing where it was coming from. Then, through a gap in the walls, behind the security dome, he spotted flecks of yellow and black, moving back and forth. He squinted, couldn't make it out.

"Zoom in," he commanded his Eye-Tab, magnifying everything

before him. What he saw frightened him: hundreds of Company soldiers marching back and forth in formation, their arms and legs in unison as they kept beat to the sound of that drum. Suddenly, the sound stopped, and they all halted, turned and saluted – the School of Economics salute. *Who were they saluting*, he wondered? What admiral lay beyond his field of vision?

He flicked off the Eye-Tab zoom and darted out of sight. He'd never seen so many Company soldiers. He'd seen small groups of soldiers doing training exercises before, keeping themselves prepared in case of an attack by anti-globalists, but this felt different, as if Gorilla Industries was preparing for war, and its only enemies, beyond those pillars of resistance – the ecological and economic terrorists – were the Company's competitor in supplying information and controlling the internet.

What are they all doing? he wondered. What was *he* doing?

He arrived at the tiny lawn at the front of his solo-home unit. His legs were shaky, and he had a tight knot in the pit of his stomach. The foreboding sight of those soldiers had reminded him, fiercely, he was breaking the rules – and breaking them in such a flagrant way. He couldn't remember ever leaving work early like this. There had been times when he'd been sick and had to go to the onsite doctor, who'd given him a jab and sent him back to work or, in the case of serious fever, sent him home to rest. Or when his father had been living with him, before he went into the home, and Gorilla Industries had begrudgingly approved an early finish on those first few nights when he tried to pacify his father's growing madness – but even that had been short-lived, as they quickly told Johnson that his father had to go.

This time, however, there was no approval and no request.

He'd just got up and left. And he could get into real trouble. It was the sort of action that could land him on a termination warning. But it was too late now. And there was also something exciting about the risks he was taking, as if Maya herself was pushing him through his fears.

He walked up the path between the manicured lawn and the garden, carefully checking to see that no one was waiting for him. He'd almost expected Security to jump out of a bush and drag him back to work. He breathed out as quietly as possible and then let himself in quickly, shutting and locking the door behind him. He was being silly and paranoid, he knew it. There were thousands of employees at Gorilla Industries; surely they wouldn't notice one going home a little early – especially with all the Company soldiers caught up in their hidden war games.

He flicked on the HV wall screen and launched Rachael to settle his nerves.

"Johnson, you are home earlier than expected."

"Yes. We were sent home early," he lied.

"Right. Well, that's good to know. Was there a reason?" she asked.

"Not sure, Rachael."

"It's nice to have you home." She was front and centre of his holo-vision, popping out from a tropical beach background, swaying from side to side like she was performing a slow dance. Since his encounter with Maya, Johnson had been less enamoured by her virtual movements – which didn't seem to capture his virile enthusiasm in the same way.

"I'm bit hungry actually, Rachael," he said.

"Do you want me to check the contents of the fridge for potential meals or order something online for you?"

"I wouldn't mind a becapo bowl, if you could arrange that," he replied.

"There is a four-star-rated becapo for $26, or a three-and-a-half-star for $21.50 with a free soft drink."

"The four star. I don't need a soft drink."

"The order has been placed and will be delivered by a Mega-Menu drone within 15 minutes."

"Thanks, Rachael. Now, can you also load up the AppChat on the HV and then split-screen it with the match? I'd like volume only on the AppChat until just before kick-off, say 14:55, and then add the volume on the match and surround sound it, please."

"Of course," she responded, and instantly the holo-vision came alive, with an advertisement filling the entire wall of his home unit. It was muted. The green window ran vertically down the left of the screen with a list of his AppChat connections.

"Please put my AppChat handle on silent, only visible to my *close-friends group*."

The names dropped off the screen. It was blank for a moment before Conrad's face appeared.

"Jay, you are back already. That was quick," Conrad said, settling into his seat.

"Yeah, I know. I didn't feel like working any more today, buddy."

"Good on you. Not sure how your employer is going to like it, though."

Johnson ignored the comment. Right now he didn't care what Gorilla Industries thought. That's what he told himself anyway.

"Is your mate, Mac, joining us for the game?" Johnson asked.

"No. He can't. He has some special Apple project that he's working on."

"Really? Do you know what it is?"

"Well, he wouldn't tell me, but I do know that they're working on something big, really big."

"A new version of the Eye-Tab?" queried Johnson.

"Bigger than that, my friend," said Conrad as he waved his hands excitedly around the screen. "Imagine an Eye-Tab merged with an artificial intelligence unit, right, with access to all the information available on the internet… but inside your brain."

"Inside your brain?"

"Yes. A chip is inserted in your head with everything your Eye-Tab or PID can access. This is then connected directly to the neurons in your brain."

"You wouldn't even need to put in a contact lens," Johnson suggested.

"No, that's right!"

"Geez, it sounds a bit scary. Not sure I want a computer in my brain."

"You, Jay, have always been a late developer when it comes to technology. Imagine the benefits: you would have access to every piece of information on the web, and your brain could use that data instantaneously; you would be a genius. Even *you* would be a genius." Conrad chuckled. "There is nothing you wouldn't know or be able to find out. Imagine what you could do, what you could achieve. Imagine the possibilities."

"Does it actually get implanted permanently in your brain, or is it just connected somehow?" asked Johnson.

"I don't know the details," replied Conrad. "It's top-secret at the moment. They're still doing testing… and I'm only guessing from what I've heard, but I assume the chip and the brain connect up and can access each other like two interconnected devices.

If you wanted to order something from a shop, then you could think of it, and it would arrive at your door within minutes. Or say... you wanted to know something – a fact or some information you required for work or whatever – then you would know it before you had time to wonder about it. And it would be like you always knew it."

Johnson shook his head. It seemed a crazy, fanciful concept, but then 10 years ago no one imagined the Dream Weaver would exist. "Do you think it could get into your brain and take over your thoughts?"

Conrad seemed to digest the question slowly, rubbing his chin before answering: "Maybe. I guess it's possible, but you also wouldn't know they were not your thoughts... so it wouldn't be a problem. They'd just seem like *your* thoughts originating in *your* mind."

An advertisement popped up on the HV, distracting them both. About a dozen tall beauties walked around in sexy underwear. They had all been surgically enhanced, with sharp cone-shaped breasts and symmetrical round bums. They wore bright-orange knickers that sucked in their hips. You could buy the underwear with a wink or a word. And there was an option to talk to the ladies – no doubt an artificial social unit with a sensual voice designed to play on the insecurities of lonely men.

"I wonder if they could plant advertisements in your brain to make you want to buy things," Johnson said as he turned his attention back to Conrad.

"Huh," Conrad said, not really listening. There was a pause, and then he went on hurriedly: "We haven't even seen the development of proper free-thinking artificial intelligence yet. I reckon this will crush the Brain Race. Who needs to develop machines with the capacity to think for themselves when you can make a human into a machine?"

Johnson had always been told the importance of technology; how robotics had created greater efficiency in the workplace. He had heard lectures at the School of Economics on Musk and Jobs and other prophets who supported these ideas. Now it appeared that humans were on the cusp of joining the computers and becoming gods, and all he wanted to do was run away and forget about it. He didn't need an Eye-Tab or a brain chip or an electric car. He didn't need drones bringing him goods, or fridges that cut up his carrots. He didn't need the AppChat or Conrad or Rachael... he just needed Maya.

"Are you alright, Johnson? You seem a little quiet."

"I am thinking about... about someone."

"Who?"

"A girl I met," Johnson answered shyly.

"Really? Tell me more," replied Conrad, his face filled with intrigue.

"I met this girl, Maya, the other week. Here at work, actually. And we went out last weekend, on Saturday night, and then we stayed together all the next day as well," Johnson added proudly.

"This is incredible, Jay. Where did you meet her?"

"We met at the cafeteria here at Gorilla Industries."

"And you asked her out? This doesn't sound like you at all," Conrad said, a cheeky grin plastered across his face.

Johnson looked away. "Sort of... She asked me out, I guess."

"Wow! That never happens. Johnson, you handsome devil! What happened?"

"Well, she just came up to me in the cafeteria and started talking."

"That's great, mate, but tell me what happened on the date. I want details." Conrad rubbed his hands together and settled into his chair.

Johnson obliged – telling Conrad about the Italian dinner and the free wine and pasta, the botanical gardens and even the strange hotel.

"A hotel," Conrad spluttered. "Did you hook up?"

Johnson grinned, the passion of that night oozing out of his pores once more.

"Come on, tell me more," Conrad pleaded. He took a long swig from the bottle in front of him.

Johnson hesitated. "Nah, I don't want to say too much, in case I jinx it." He got up from the couch and got himself a beer.

"Come on, Jay. I am your oldest friend."

"Well, em, yeah..." He sat down on his couch and looked up at the screen. "We did it a few times, actually."

"Ha! I knew it. How did you perform? I mean, it's been a while for you, hasn't it?" Conrad sniggered.

"It went okay. But it was incredible just being with her – lying in bed, holding her, being with her. She is really beautiful. She was born in the Latin Territories, and she has this amazing brown hair and this perfect soft skin that felt like..." he paused, thinking, unable to find the right word.

"Send me a picture," Conrad interrupted.

"I don't have one."

"Come on! What's her AppChat handle then?"

"She doesn't use AppChat. She's not really into social media."

"Surely she has an About-Face profile. What's her name? I'll see if I can find her."

"Her name is Maya, and that's all I know. You won't find her.

As I said, she's not into social media." He secretly hoped Conrad would find her, and then he could send her a message.

"Sounds like you're in love, Jay."

Johnson sipped his beer and lay back on the couch, while Conrad waited quietly for a response. Johnson eventually replied: "I don't know, Conrad... I want to see her all the time."

"Really?"

"Maybe, yeah."

"You haven't been in love with anyone since that girl Rachael from school broke your heart... and your hologram of Rachael, of course." Conrad laughed. "But that is really just the same girl."

"I haven't even thought about Rachael," Johnson said defensively. "Although she looks a bit like her."

"Ha! Of course,' Conrad shot back. "You were a mess for years because of Rachael. After she left the school, you were never the same. I know because I was there. It wasn't your fault, but it still left you a broken man. I mean, I've been picking up the pieces ever since." Conrad looked down at his hands, and then added quietly, "I hope you're not going to let that happen again, are you?"

"I don't know. We just met. I haven't seen her all week."

"Well, why not?" Conrad's expression changed immediately to one of righteous indignation.

"I was waiting for her, I guess. I didn't know what to do, how to contact her. I can't find her on About-Face or any social media sites. I've looked everywhere."

"Ha-ha, so you did look for her on About-Face."

Johnson nodded. His face went red. There was a pause and Johnson hoped this was the end of the conversation. He was about to start talking about the grand final and who was going to win, when Conrad intervened: "But don't you work with her?"

"Yes, I do, and I haven't seen her at work either,' Johnson replied. "I've been to the cafeteria every day this week looking for her, and I wait at the bottom of the lifts after work each night, but I haven't seen her anywhere."

Conrad gave a shake of his head. "Did she tell you where she works? What department?"

"Sort of... I guess. I've got an idea anyway," he replied, then added, "Well, she told me the floor she works on."

"Go and see her then," demanded Conrad.

Johnson hesitated. "Do you think so?"

"Oh, Johnson, what are you doing? She wants you to find her. Why else did she tell you where you could find her?"

Johnson sat considering the proposition. "Alright, I will. I will go and see her," he said finally.

"Tomorrow, Johnson. First thing," Conrad snapped. "You have to strike in the morning while the solar panels are charged. Otherwise, you'll just put it off."

"Right. Yeah, I'll go see her tomorrow. Thanks, Conrad," he added. It was at moments like these that he really appreciated his best friend. His confidence was infectious.

"Ah, this is fantastic. Cheers!" Conrad thrust his bottle into the air, and they pretended to clink them together as if they were sitting side by side in a pub.

"This game better be starting soon," Conrad said. "You think you can concentrate for a few hours on this game and not on... what's her name again?"

"Maya."

"Yeah, Maya."

Johnson nodded. "My game volume should be coming on at any moment," he said.

"Who are you going for?" Conrad asked.

"The Globals, of course. Can't let the Zucks win. I hate them... Those bastards! What they did to my father. I'll never forgive them for that."

"Your father worked for them, yeah?"

"Thirty-two years all up, between About U and About-Face, after they merged with Facebook, and they didn't give him a company pension at the end of it all."

"That's terrible," Conrad replied, shaking his head.

"I know. Don't get me started. And that's why he's in a Government home, poor bugger, and I can't see him." Johnson felt his eyes welling up with tears. "I just want to make sure he's doing okay, and give him a hug..."

The sounds of screeching brakes filled the room. Johnson looked up at the advert for one of the companies with driverless cars available for hire on the car-grid. It showed a reel of horrible footage from motor accidents before the driverless car was invented.

"Turn it down a bit, Rachael," Johnson yelled.

The ads were followed by the betting odds. A beautiful woman appeared on the HV. She moved sensually across the holographic wall screen as she announced the odds for each of the teams, and first and last goal scorers, as well as prices for other games and sports being played across the globe:

"If you want in-play odds, make sure you say 'BET' at any time during the game. Today's special is on any new haircuts or tattoos for the players, game length to the nearest second, and number of times the ball goes out. There is also a free player-scandal bet, open for 12 months after the game.

"If you are using your Eye-Tab, make sure you click 'STAR' to see

the live in-play odds and have access to real-time statistics for every player. This feature is brought to you by Always-a-Winner – Always the place to bet and always the place to win."

"You going to place a bet tonight, Jay?" Conrad asked, his eyes focused on the odds scrolling across the bottom of the screen.

"Nah, don't really want to," Johnson murmured.

"Come on, mate. A few bets to keep it interesting," Conrad implored. "The Chargers aren't playing, remember."

"I don't see the point," Johnson replied calmly.

The teams ran onto the field and Johnson settled into his couch. He thought about Maya. The way he felt when he was with her. The excitement she encapsulated in her smooth round shoulders. The way she saw the world; it was as if it were her world, to do what she wanted. He felt inspired. Tomorrow he would go and see her. He couldn't take another day without her. He had to see her, to hear her confident voice, to touch her perfect skin... to know how she felt about him. He would head to the 112th floor.

11.

He hadn't gone to find Maya yet. He knew Conrad would be disappointed in him, but he couldn't bring himself to do it. He was too scared of rejection: of Maya, of everything.

I need to go to the toilet, he thought. He got up from his desk and walked down the corridor to the all-sex bathroom, promising himself that he would go down to the 112th floor and try to find her as soon as he was finished – as he'd done after every coffee that morning and every time he'd finalised an edit.

His urine was a luminous yellow colour, as if he was a resident of the Bendowyne fallout zone, but the truth was less sinister: he took too many Vitastrength mineral supplements to avoid getting sick. It was something he'd done for years, ever since Gorilla Industries had abolished sick leave.

As he wandered back to his desk, he saw Lylo coming towards him. Lylo had an androgynous face with a sharp nose, pronounced cheekbones, short, thin lips thickened slightly by tattoo ink, and dyed blond hair cut short – a classic look for one who did not identify as a man or a woman.

"How are you?" asked Johnson.

"Okay, I guess," Lylo replied, "although I'm a bit worried about our jobs."

"Why, what happened?"

"Nothing has happened yet. But I heard a rumour that they are going to automate our department."

"What, the whole thing?" Johnson queried as he rubbed nervously at the back of his neck.

Lylo nodded, then flicked hir blond fringe out of hir eyes. "Yeah, the entire Information Editing Unit, if my source is correct."

"Geez. I didn't know we were in the firing line. They always said they needed us for the creative side. I thought the automated systems couldn't do that yet."

"Well, they must be learning," Lylo replied with a cackle. "I heard that as early as next year they will begin to phase us out."

"Damn this place!" Johnson said angrily.

"Yeah, I know. What a shame for all of us; a real shit fight. But we should have expected it," Lylo said with a shudder.

"Yeah, I guess. Thanks for telling me."

"Sure. Now, I've really got to go to the bathroom." Lylo began to move down the corridor. "See you later."

Johnson stood for a moment, in shock. He should have known. It could just be a rumour, but even if it didn't happen next year, it would happen eventually. It was inevitable, like the rising tides of the ocean. He trudged back to his desk, logged on to his desktop and stared at the screen. He didn't want to edit the piece in front of him, not after what he'd just heard. Surely they couldn't get rid of everyone. He felt nauseous. He knew he had to go and find Maya. It was now or never.

As he went down the lift to her department, he considered the possibilities: (1) She was elated to see him and rushed out to hug him in a moment of passion; (2) She was happy to see him and they used this opportunity to arrange their next meeting; (3) She didn't care either way; (4) She didn't want to see him; or

(5) She was most upset and annoyed by his presence, and asked him to leave and never visit again.

He thought about their weekend together – the way she had touched his arm and kissed him goodbye. There were feelings there, he knew it. He just had to trust his instincts.

The lift stopped. "112th floor. Have a nice day."

Johnson got out and walked along a narrow white corridor. He reached a doorway at the end and entered. Inside was a reception desk.

"Please identify the person you would like to visit," said the automated receptionist.

Johnson leaned forward. "Maya."

"Please identify the person you would like to visit," the voice repeated. "Say 'help' if you require customer assistance."

"Help," Johnson said tentatively.

"Please wait."

Johnson leaned against the desk and began to sweat. It took a few minutes. Eventually, a middle-aged woman emerged from a small gap in the wall opposite. She was wearing a long black skirt, white shoes, and a white shirt with large metal buttons. She was plump and had greying, shoulder-length hair. There was a strong aroma of perfume, which made him gag a little.

"Can I help you?" she asked in a high-pitched, grating voice.

"Yes. I am looking for an employee who works on this floor."

"The employee's name?"

"Maya."

"Ah! Right," said the lady. "Would you hold on a moment," she added, turning her back to him.

"Sure!"

Johnson shook with excitement and fear. This was the moment of his destiny.

The lady took a few steps away and then stopped and turned back to face him. She looked at him curiously. "What's your name? Are you an employee here?"

"Yes, I'm Johnson, from the Information Editing Unit."

He stood silently as she scanned him. "Thank you, Johnson. You can never be too careful these days."

"Absolutely!"

"Give me a minute," she added. She walked back through the gap between the walls, and then through a doorway on the other side. He heard her mumbling to someone.

Maybe it's Maya, he thought. He wondered how she would react when she came through the doorway and saw him standing there. *She will be coming through any moment now,* he thought as he rubbed his hand over his shaved head, feeling the short and stubbly bristles of hair. But no one came.

He could still hear the lady speaking but couldn't make out what she was saying. He crept between the two walls, through the doorway, and peeked inside. He saw a large open-plan area similar to his department. Behind this was a plate-glass wall, and then what looked like a restricted area with gasmasks, glass beakers, rubber hoses and other equipment. Around the edges were sinks and pipes and various cleansing and burning devices. He could see two people in white coats peering into the glowing hole of a large white cylinder. Next to this, yellow, blue and red dots were pulsed by lasers onto a wall.

The lady from reception saw him and jumped.

"Sorry, yes," she spluttered. "He has just come in. Okay. Yes. I will tell him that. Thanks."

She walked towards Johnson. "Sorry, sir, this is a restricted zone."

"Oh, right. I wasn't sure if you wanted me to follow you or not," he said, blushing.

She bristled. "I would have said *that*."

He wasn't going to give up now. He had come this far. "So is Maya here then?" he said firmly, in a voice he didn't recognise. It felt good, just the act of standing there, refusing to bend to the authority of the walls around him.

"There is no Maya here." Her voice was stern. She looked at him gravely.

"What do you mean?"

"She doesn't work here."

"When did she leave?" asked a stunned Johnson.

The lady looked away.

"She never worked here. There has never been a Maya in this department," she sighed.

"Can you check again," he pleaded, his voice faltering.

She hesitated, then gave Johnson a stern look. "I have checked twice and have also checked with Human Resources."

"This is the Research Laboratory, isn't it?" he stuttered, grasping on to the faint hope he may be in the wrong place.

"I am going to have to ask you to leave."

"But I work here."

"Yes, but this is a restricted area, even for employees." She walked right up to him, standing less than a foot away, her lips pursed, the red lipstick smudging slightly.

"Okay, fine," he said, submitting to her will.

She led him back to the reception desk.

"Hold on." She held up her hand, so her small palm was right in front of Johnson's eyes and put her other hand on her earpiece. "Yes, I will do that, sir. I'll send him down to you."

Johnson stood still, listening, hardly daring to breathe. She looked him in the eyes, a smug grin on her face. "I have been asked by the Human Resources Manager... well, actually, he has requested you go see him."

"What? When?"

"Now," she said, pointing at the door.

Johnson sensed an opportunity. "I'll head there right now then." He turned around and bolted out of the office.

12.

As Johnson jumped off the lift, he saw the Human Resources hologram light up against the wall – a human pyramid, signifying each person's integral part of the structure. To Johnson, it just looked like people standing on the shoulders of other people, using them to get closer to the top.

The department took up the entire fourth floor. It was an open-plan office with cubicles in clumps like tufts of tundra grass. Around the perimeter were small glassed-in offices. The desks were pushed up against the windows, ensuring the managers could keep an eye on the screens of their employees, make sure they were always working. Not that they needed that nowadays – the computers monitored every second of work, tracking logged hours and efficiency across each hour. The windows themselves were made from reinforced glass to curb the suicide rate. It was good for morale to keep those percentages low, and good ammunition for the Marketing Team – remind customers that Gorilla Industries was an 'employer that cared'.

Johnson tapped his fingers against his leg and paced up and down. He was approached by a pretty young girl with red hair, freckles and high cheekbones.

"Can I help you?" she asked.

"I'm not sure," Johnson answered. "I was asked to come and see the Human Resources Manager."

"Your name?"

"Johnson. From Information Editing."

"Mr Melville will be with you shortly. If you would take a seat," she said, pointing with a slender finger to a mustard-coloured couch behind him.

Melville! Johnson couldn't believe it. He felt an immediate sense of relief. He stopped pacing, took a deep breath and sat down.

"Would you like a coffee or tea?" the girl asked.

"Ah, no thanks," replied Johnson, who was still twitchy from the three coffees he'd had that morning. "It's nice to be able to order from a real person, though," he added. He saw 'Mango' on the name badge on her lapel and read it aloud. Underneath her name was 'Employee of the Month – Human Resources'.

She smiled. "We like to give a personal touch here in Human Resources, for humans are our best resource."

"It is definitely better than the Robot Resources Department," he said with a chuckle.

She laughed awkwardly, and then left him to wait. He felt relieved. He was right to come. Conrad was right. Everything was going to be fine. Melville would lead him to Maya and all would be well.

After a few minutes, Mango returned.

"Please follow me, Mr Johnson," she said.

He got up and followed her to an office at the far corner of the room. "In here," she said, gesturing him inward.

Johnson thanked her and headed inside the office. It was bigger than the others. Raymond Melville sat behind a desk, tapping away at an old-style keyboard, his grey hair draped across his forehead, his matching grey eyes burrowed into the digital screen before him. Johnson cleared his throat.

12.

"Sit down," Melville barked. He continued to type without looking up. "I can't use these damn voice-based text programs. It comes out all wrong," said Melville. He eventually looked up and stared at Johnson. "Now, let's get straight to the point, Johnson. Do you know why you're here?"

Johnson hesitated. "Yes, I am looking for a colleague."

Melville stopped Johnson with a flick of his hand. "We can't have employees leaving early Johnson, not without permission. You should know that."

"I, ah, don't know... I am not sure what you mean."

Melville pressed some keys on his old black keyboard. "Ah yes, here it is. We have a report." He pointed to something on his screen. "Yesterday, at exactly 14:07, you arrived at your home unit in the Employee Village."

"Huh?"

"Johnson, Johnson," he said, shaking his head. "I like you a lot, but this is a breach of company policy. And on a Saturday too, when the Company already lets you leave work four hours early."

"Sorry, I thought I was coming here for something else."

"Don't worry about anything else, Johnson. We are talking about an employment infraction here, which will not look good on your record, especially now."

Johnson shook his head. His face began to flush.

"I will be more specific. Please answer me carefully. You accept that you were at work yesterday, correct?"

Johnson nodded.

"And you didn't request leave or have an 'exceptional circumstances' early mark?"

"No."

"And then you left work and returned home at exactly 14:07?"

"I am not sure of the time." Johnson looked down at his feet, wondering how the slum they knew. He was sure he had left himself logged on to avoid this.

"We have a report here from your Home Intelligence Unit confirming the time." Melville turned the screen towards Johnson. There was an online report with the six days of the working week, and his departure and arrival times for each of those days.

Rachael! There was some other information on the screen, but he was so angry he couldn't read it. Rachael was spying on him. How could she? After all he had done for her. Yet here she was, sending information back to his employer about his daily routine, telling them what time he arrived home, what time he left. She probably listed all the websites he searched and his conversations on AppChat too. There was only football talk with Conrad but, still, it was an invasion of whatever privacy he had left. How could he be so foolish as to trust her? "I can't believe Rachael would do this me," he said softly.

"It's alright, Johnson," Melville said with a hint of tenderness. "This is just standard protocol."

Johnson gathered himself together. "Okay, I did leave early yesterday," he replied. He took a deep breath, ready to take his medicine. "I'm sorry, Raymond. I was tired and stressed and needed to go home..."

Melville looked unconvinced.

"It was a bad day," continued Johnson. "I'm sorry. It won't happen again."

"Look, Johnson. I like you. I want to help you. These things happen. You made a mistake, and you accept that. But in future you need to get leave. You need to get approval. It is company policy.

"Here." Melville passed him a tissue and then went on: "We all work for Gorilla Industries, and we have to follow the rules."

"So do I get a warning or anything like that?" Johnson asked.

"No. I am not going to do that. You have been here for over nine years and have never been in any trouble. Your attendance record is good, except for a brief period some years back, when you missed a few days of work and had some... absences."

"Oh, right. Yes. That was when my father was staying, before he went into the home."

"Right. Apart from that period, you have been an exemplary employee and, for the most part, your manager has written good things about your editing work. And the paid content you have created seems to have pleased most of our advertisers. So we don't want to lose you, but we need to make sure this doesn't happen again. Understand?"

Johnson nodded.

"Remember, Johnson, Gorilla Industries has been good to you. We have given you a place to live, and we pay you above the minimum wage if you include the subsidised part of your rent and the extras included in your home unit. You should remember that going forward, and make sure you repay the Company in kind by committing to being the best employee, the best Information Editor, you can be."

"Yes. I will do that," Johnson replied. For a moment, he considered asking Melville about the job automations, and whether Lylo was correct in saying the Information Editing Unit was going to be replaced... but now wasn't the time.

Melville leaned forward. "You will re-pledge your allegiance to Gorilla Industries."

Johnson nodded, his last vestige of strength waning like the last days of the original moon's cycle.

"Do you swear on the Economy?" Melville asked, a closed fist rubbing forebodingly against an open palm.

"I do," Johnson answered formally, his head bowed in deference.

"I will also be deducting three hours of pay for the time you missed, and a further five hours penalty."

Johnson was just happy to avoid a termination warning. "Thanks, Raymond. I really appreciate your leniency," he said. He'd expected at least an infraction notice, and to have his sins broadcast whenever he arrived at the office or went through the gate into the Employee Village.

"No problem, Johnson. As I said before, I like you and want you here for the long haul. Was there anything else you needed?"

It came flooding back - the reason he came. Johnson felt a surge of energy as if he'd just gulped down a blue electrolyte popper. "Yes, there is, actually," he said. This was his last chance to find her.

"Go on," Melville said, frowning slightly.

Johnson hesitated. His heart skipped a beat. "There is a lady I met." He looked up at Melville, who was staring at his screen again. "A fellow employee, actually," Johnson corrected, "who I'm looking to find."

"Is this the employee you were looking for on the 112th floor with Trisha?"

"I was told she would be on that floor," Johnson replied.

Melville spoke calmly: "Who is this employee, Johnson? And what does she mean to you?"

"Her name is Maya, and I think she works in the Research Laboratory. At least that's what she told me."

"Any other information you have about her?"

He shook his head.

Johnson watched as Melville tapped away at his computer. "No, nothing here," he said. "Perhaps there is another name you have for her?"

"That's all I know," Johnson replied sadly.

Melville tapped on his keyboard again, his eyes scrolling down the computer screen methodically. "No, nothing. I am sorry, Johnson. We don't have any Mayas here at Gorilla Industries. Are you sure she works here?"

"Yes, I know she does," Johnson blurted out. He was hit by a rush of anger and panic – a strange mix that seemed to dissolve the last of his inhibitions. "I know she does, and I saw you with her."

"What's that?"

Melville stared at Johnson; the glimmer of a man who once liked to fight appeared.

"I saw you with her in the cafeteria, a few weeks ago," Johnson explained. "Her name is Maya, and she has short, dark hair and brown eyes. She wasn't wearing the uniform..." Johnson faltered for a moment, not knowing if he should go on. "And she started working here that day I saw her with you... so you must have hired her," said Johnson finally.

Melville twitched. "Johnson, I have never heard of this Maya. I haven't hired anyone in months, and I don't like your attitude."

Johnson jumped up, forgetting himself, forgetting where he was and who he was talking to. "You liar!" he screamed.

Melville stood up and jabbed a finger at Johnson. "Did you just call me a liar?"

The courage that had driven him to this point quickly turned to fear and his heart rattled in his chest. He became acutely aware of the power imbalance between them. He could feel it in the air, like a dog challenging the alpha male then realising too late what he has done.

Melville could sack him, but it didn't matter. It meant nothing now without Maya. "I saw you with her," he whimpered.

"There is no Maya here. And I am going to have to write you up, Johnson."

Johnson flopped down in the chair. "I am sorry," he said, his voice faltering. "I am so sorry. I just don't know what to do." He thought of Maya. *Where are you?* he wondered. Had she abandoned him? He sat in silence, looking down at his lap, unable to face Melville. The office around him dimmed, a haze of grey encircled him, beat down on him, as if he had found himself lost and alone in a wild storm.

"I am giving you a termination warning. I want you to leave my office and go back to the Information Editing Unit," snapped Melville. "Think about how you have behaved. And get this silly Maya girl out of your head. She doesn't exist. She never did. Now leave."

Johnson stood up. His head pounded. The room whirred around him. He turned around and stumbled out of Melville's office. He felt people around him staring. He didn't care. He was lost. He was dizzy. He was hurt.

"Maya," he cried.

He started dry-retching in the lift, trying to vomit up everything – the whole overwhelming moment, the nauseating energy of unrequited love, and the bleak pain of his despondency. It wouldn't come up, and he heaved up nothingness, unable to stop until the lift reached his floor.

13.

"Here," she said, handing the PID to Camus. As usual, he was sitting at his desk with the LAN/S-pod, surrounded by a multitude of flickering screens.

"What's on it?" he said, glancing up.

"Everything I could get. His login details, not the password, obviously – you will need to get that – but I got his thumbprints and managed a face scan as well."

"Okay, thanks."

He took hold of the PID, placed it carefully beside him and attached it to the LAN/S-pod with a thin grey cable.

She stretched her shoulders. She took a long, deep breath, was hit by the acrid smell of the lake again. It was awful, got right in the nose, but it was worth it to be safely out of the city.

"Will that be enough?" she asked.

"I'm not sure. There are some issues," said Camus. "I'll see if I can reconstruct the password from the back end, work it against the background information we have… but that may take some time. And I'll need to see what security they are using for their editors."

"Maybe Eileen could help with that?" Una suggested, although she knew Eileen was a long way away, and from what she'd heard, Eileen liked to stay offline, disconnected, and only took face-to-face visits in the café.

Camus didn't say anything, then muttered: "I don't think she'd be too happy if she knew who we used."

"What's that?" she asked.

Camus didn't reply, just put his head down into his screen and began working his magic.

A few hours passed. She sat down in the kitchen, her foot tapping hurriedly on the slowly-decaying vinyl floor. *It is good to be back,* she thought. It was good to get out there and do her part, but also nice to be back in the relative safety of the house, despite the smell. She just hoped she was making a difference.

"How's Parks going?" she asked, disturbing Camus from his work. "Have you heard from her?"

"She's arranged things," replied Camus without looking up.

"That's good, I suppose." She felt sorry for Parks, for what she was giving up for this, but she was dedicated; a true hero of their cause. Una wished Parks was there now, and she could tell her about Johnson. He was only a mark, necessary for their mission, but she had grown fond of him in a funny, hard-to-explain kind of way.

The door opened. Lenmar strutted in. His trim bony face covered in dark brown stubble, which was much darker than the brown curls on the top of his head.

"Una Maya," he bellowed out in his affectionate way. He walked over and gave her a hug.

"Just Una now," she said. "I left Maya at the door when I left Gorilla Industries."

Lenmar laughed. "You've finished there then, well done."

"What have you been doing? She asked.

"I've been testing the cam-bots. Preparing to send them in to the home," Lenmar said proudly. "They are almost ready to be let loose, hey Camus?" He walked across the room to where Camus was typing furiously on a hologram typewriter.

Camus looked up and gave a nod. "Hopefully they can get

inside without a hitch," he said.

"How are things looking on this end? Have you found a way inside yet?"

"Working on it," came the curt response. "But they have extra security for the Information Editing Unit," he added.

"What does that mean?" Lenmar asked, with a furrowed brow. "Can we still get access and post the content?"

"No. I don't think so. Not yet, anyway. Una's got a lot of stuff for us. We can bypass the login and the eye scan, and even the thumbprint, but there also a live scan that reads DNA."

"Well surely we can get some of this Information Editor's DNA then. Or we can go back and get some."

Una jumped in: "He used my PID, so there would be DNA on the screen."

Camus said: "We have some already, and I'm trying that, but it's not working. I think we need it matching to live blood cells, or living tissue. The online scan seems to read their DNA in real time against the living cells. Basically, from what I can deduce, you can only access the back end of the network if you have an editor with you in person, with a beating heart, who can then bypass the live scan while simultaneously logged on."

Lenmar turned to Una: "Didn't Eileen mention any of this to you?"

She hesitated, unsure if she had missed something when she'd gone to see her at the Emerald Café. Eileen had provided a lot of background information about Gorilla Industries, and got her in contact with the right people, but there had been no mention of having to bring back an editor.

Camus piped up: "This is only on the latest security system. It was after her time, unfortunately."

Lenmar stood there for a moment, deep in thought. He rubbed his eye. "Well, we'll just have to bring him in. We can beat the live read by getting him here with us, right?"

Camus nodded.

Lenmar went on: "Easy! We get him here, then we go live." He looked directly at Una. "What's his name again?"

"Johnson. But I'm not sure he'd–"

"Can you get him out here?"

"What," Una stammered. "He is back at Gorilla Industries. He still works there."

"Well, you need to get back in there," said Lenmar firmly. "Are you compromised?"

"No, no." She hesitated. "I don't think so."

"It's an easy choice then." Lenmar looked at her with his fierce, burning eyes, as if he were peering into her very core.

She hesitated.

"We need this, Una!"

She nodded.

"YESSS!" he shouted. "You are a true warrior, Una."

"I guess I will have to be Maya again," she added.

"For the greater good," Lenmar said, winking.

"Yeah, I know," she replied. She felt a flush of heat in her face. "But what are you going to do with him afterwards?" she added.

Lenmar turned away. "Whatever we have to," he said as he rubbed at his mop of curly hair. He leaned in to help Camus, his long torso cutting across the room, cutting through their conversation.

She needed to say more, much more, but spoke in rapid spurts: "He's a good man. I don't want to bring him back here so we can use him and then spit him out again. I don't want to sacrifice another person for the cause. We are meant to be saving lives here, you know, not making things worse."

Lenmar faced her again. "You know this is important, maybe the most important thing we have ever done. We need to expose what's going on. You knew there would be risks and... umm... difficult choices when you started out. Things we have to do for the greater good. So people can know the truth - the real truth, not the truth that is spooned into their mouths."

"But not this! You know what will happen."

"His is not much of a life anyway," Camus added.

She had tears in her eyes and was about to storm off.

"Come on, Una," Lenmar pleaded. He stood up to face her again. "Think of what Parks is doing, and what her grandmother is doing, for this, for the greater good. We can't back out now. And there is no one else. You have a gift for this... we need you to get him here."

He was right. She had no choice in the matter, especially after the sacrifices the others had made. But it broke her heart to do it to Johnson. There was innocence in him... he was like a mole living out in a field, and she didn't want to be the one to take the plough to that field, to make it suitable for new growth, but also destroy him in the process.

"And when this shit goes down, you'll be glad that he's out of there, out of that battery cage of a place."

She eventually relented. "Alright then, I'll go back in and get him." She turned around and headed towards the door, eyes on the floor, stinging with sadness, torn between a need to protect Johnson and her duty to the cause.

She reached the door and turned back. "Just promise me that you'll do what you can for him. Don't throw him to the wolves after it's done."

PART III

1.

The van brakes and he slides forward, his body squashed against the front of the cage. It turns in a long, wide arc. The armed police sitting opposite him lift their guns. They jostle from side to side as if gearing up for movement. Their faces are covered. He wishes he could see their eyes, and perhaps glean from their expressions what fate awaits him.

His head still hurts with a dull throbbing at the back. *Have they done serious damage?* he wonders. *Will he even survive this ordeal?* What he has witnessed over the last few days has left him without hope. Deflated. Lost.

The van inches forward, then stops. The engine is still running. He hears a creaking noise, a click, and then people talking. Two of them. He can't make out what they are saying. He tries to listen, pressing his ear to the side of the van, hoping the sound will carry through the metal.

He hears some muffled words: "We have one for you..."

The other voice responds, says something that ends with "down there".

The first voice again, clear this time: "Where do we collect payment?"

Then there's some stuff he doesn't understand. Some grunts, and another creaking sound. The van moves forward, drives a short distance, then turns and reverses. It stops. The engine cuts. The police soldiers jump out of their seats, guns in hand. The cage door swings open, and he is fished out with a hook. He tries to crawl with the hook still attached to his shirt, dragging him forward. At the cage door, he is grabbed gruffly by one of the police soldiers, before a second one latches on and heaves him out.

The van door opens, and he is hit by a blinding light. *Am I in heaven?* he wonders... before the world slowly emerges around him.

2.

Johnson looked over at his green duffel bag. It was lying carefully by his bed, out of view of the wall screen camera, and packed with all his essential gear. He peered carefully out the tiny window above his bed. It was still dark outside. He wondered if he was going to go through with it. It was madness. But what choice did he have? They had made the decision for him.

He had barely slept at all – he kept tossing and turning, flipping the pillow over, throwing off the covers and pulling them back up, unsure if he was hot or cold or just too anxious to regulate his body heat.

He thought about yesterday: trying to find Maya; reaching a dead end at the Research Laboratory and then again with Human Resources; calling Melville a liar, then returning to his desk, waiting all afternoon for the dreaded *termination warning* to flash up on his screen. He couldn't think about anything else.

One question kept turning over in his head: if she didn't work at Gorilla Industries, where could she be? For a moment, he even considered the possibility that this was all in his head, part of a dream he'd conjured on his Dream Weaver. Or, worse, he was trapped in a game of *SimLife* and this whole series of events was just being played out in virtual reality. She was just a chip on a computer inserted into his brain, pre-programmed into a world of his own making. It was all possible, but a part of him knew she was real. It was the same part that knew he was real: his core, or soul, or whatever people wanted to call it, where he felt the truth of things in a world in which truth and reality were as malleable as DNA.

The more he thought about it, the more he believed she must have been terminated by Gorilla Industries. Or, worse, something had happened to her, and they were covering it up. The way the lady on the 112th floor had handled his request for information – hesitating, unsure what to say, as if she knew of Maya but couldn't admit to it. The way Melville had reacted, pretending he'd never met Maya, lying to his face, even though Johnson had seen them together in the cafeteria when she first started the job. It didn't make sense, none of it did. But he knew he had to do something about it. He couldn't leave Maya out there, wherever she was, alone or in some sort of difficulty. He was going to find her.

Yesterday, he had turned Rachael off as soon as he'd walked in the door. He didn't want to speak to her, not after she had reported him to management for leaving work early. He muted her as she welcomed him home, then walked straight over to the small black box in the corner and switched off her power supply unit. That way, she couldn't send him alerts or reminders or messages or contact him, nor could she track him or tell management of his movements again. And with that switch, she was gone from his life. It felt like the day at the hospital when the doctors turned off the life-support machine for his mother. In both moments, he felt relief that it was over: his mother, because he couldn't stand the pain she was going through as her cells destroyed themselves; his Home Intelligence Unit, because he wanted her out of his life forever.

He had packed his bag quietly, closing the door to his bedroom, as he stuffed each item into his duffel bag – including a hooded jumper, some spare clothes and other essentials, and an old standard-issue Gorilla Industries cap which they'd given to him during his orientation week, which he'd barely worn since.

He'd gone into the bathroom to get his toiletries, when he spotted his Company-issued tablets: four containers of pills, all with different properties, all designed for the purpose of keeping him at optimum level for the job. He initially grabbed all four vials and put them in his bag – just to be on the safe side – but then took them out. He didn't need them. They were part of the problem. He didn't even know who he was without them. But letting them go proved difficult too. In the end, he took the bottle of multivitamins for his health; and the Pep-Me-Up pills in case he needed a boost.

He had also packed the old tablet device his father had given him, and its charger. The battery didn't last long, but it was his, and could be hooked up to the internet through wi-fi. It was not as sophisticated and easy to use as the Eye-Tab, but he didn't need that now anyway.

And with that thought, he strode purposefully back to the bathroom and peered into the mirror. He leaned forward, held open his left eyelid with his left hand, and slowly pulled off the Eye-Tab. It stuck for a moment on his pupil – it had been a few months since he'd last taken it out – but he plucked up the courage and yanked off the diaphanous lens like a used Band-Aid. Then he flushed it, triumphantly, down the toilet.

"Goodbye Rachael. Goodbye Gorilla Industries," he whispered to the disappearing water.

He thought about using the Dream Weaver one last time – a dream with Maya, or a flashback with his family, before his mum had died, when he was still young, and the family was happy and living together in relative harmony. His brother, the athlete, running around the yard, chucking tennis balls at him in the hope that he would stop running and face him in a rumble; his father, out in the garden with the hose, watering the flowers, trying his best to keep the place filled with colours and smells; his mother, cooking lasagne for the family, cooking too much as always, calling them all in when it was ready, and watching proudly as her family filled the seats around the big wooden table.

But these were memories in his head. Did he really need the Dream Weaver to re-create them? Who knew if Gorilla Industries was downloading his dreams too? They could easily access the data on the Dream Weaver. The thought infuriated him. He didn't want them to see any of it. His memories were his alone. He didn't have much that was his. Everything he knew or thought, every idea he created, was downloaded onto a device and stored there for safekeeping, his brain fused with Rachael and his Eye-Tab and the internet. But he still had his memories – even if he remembered things a little differently to how they may have been – and he wasn't going to let anyone access these again.

3.

Morning eventually came – slowly, as if he was watching a worm edge across a footpath. He showered and put on his Gorilla Industries work clothes. He wanted to be as inconspicuous as possible when he left. He didn't feel hungry but forced down a couple of biscuits.

He opened the front door. He stood at the doorway with the bag over his shoulder and looked back through the solo-unit he'd called home for more than nine years.

There had been some good times, especially watching football with Conrad over the HV, but he couldn't remember ever having anyone to visit, except maybe Eileen, and the few months when his father had stayed, but for the rest of those years, it had been him alone with his Home Intelligence Unit.

How strangely isolating it was living in his home unit amid thousands of other home units inhabited by other employees of Gorilla Industries, within an Employee Village, which was surrounded by other compounds and other employee villages, and the Capital City Business District, and then suburb after suburb – housing the wealthiest elites down to the bottom rung of renters – in concentric circles until they reached the slums that surrounded them all in a city of 36 million people. Yet they were all strangers to him, living out their own lives, some right next door, too scared to even talk to one another, or get involved in one another's lives, as if this was the biggest sin of them all.

He walked down the footpath, past his garden that was maintained by the Company. He leaned down and smelled one of the flowers. It didn't have any scent. He touched it. It felt soft and gentle and almost plant-like, but it was synthetic, of course. He spat on the ground. "Damn this place!"

He walked briskly up towards the tower, scanning through the gate and his daily greeting, and then in and up the elevator to the 165th floor. He headed straight to his computer, keeping his eyes in front, avoiding the other employees in his unit, all while trying to shake off the fear that seemed intent on beating through his chest and out into the sterile office around him. He logged on to his computer system and then left without a word, not daring to look back as he darted down the hall to the lift. He grabbed the old, unused work cap from his bag and put it on his head, pulling it down low over his eyes and ears. He was almost in a daze as he got in the lift, hardly thinking about what he was doing, going through the motions as if he were just another bot and all this had been pre-programmed into his hard drive.

As he reached the bottom, he looked around to make sure it was clear, then glided over to the reception room in the corner. He peered inside. He could see the giant gorilla face staring down at him with its hard black eyes, reminding him this was a no-go zone for employees, reminding him of his servitude to the great Company. He could also see the door to the outside world. He hadn't walked in or out of that door since his job interview all those years ago.

He waited, unsure exactly of his next move. He could risk it and try to scan out, but he had no idea how, and it would surely alert his employer to his departure. Would they even care that he had left? Or would it make things easier – they could avoid another termination, and another employee dragged off by the Company soldiers. But he had to go, that's all he knew.

Then, as if willed into action by his need, the door slid open. A man in a suit began to walk through. *This is my chance,* thought Johnson, as his arms and legs pulsated with natural adrenaline. He sprang from his position, like a leopard, and bolted through the reception area. And just as the doors were about to shut, he darted past the man and outside into the fresh air. He felt a flood of excitement rush through him, as if breaking the rules was a new form of feel-good tablet.

The excitement was short-lived, for now he was on the outside and had to get going, get into town, with the reality of his choices closing in like the surrounding colossal skyscrapers.

It was too early to go to the restaurant, so Johnson decided to pass some time in a café on the mall. Time seemed to hold in the air, rigid and unmoving, while Johnson paced around the café, not knowing where to sit. He eventually found a seat in the corner and ordered a coffee from the computer ordering system in the centre of the table. A few minutes later, the coffee arrived on a toy train that ran down tracks between the tables.

He took a sip and blinked for his Eye-Tab to come on. Nothing happened. He suddenly remembered peeling the lens off his eye last night and tossing it into the toilet, and, for a moment, was a little annoyed by the inconvenience, despite knowing, deep down, it was necessary. He got out his tablet and hooked it up to the wi-fi, then watched the customary pop-up ads, then scrolled through to the Newslink website.

There was an article about the arrests of various anti-globalists for an explosion in the Capital. It listed their names with a summary of their evil deeds and past crimes against the Economy. It was followed by the story of a planned ecoterrorist plot on the Denseng Headquarters that had been foiled by a joint operation of the State Police and the Home Security Office.

Johnson looked around nervously, acutely aware that Home Security officers could be anywhere. He then turned his attention back to the information appearing on his screen, reading through slivers of news in a mostly futile attempt to waylay his growing paranoia.

There was further tension between the Re-Formed Soviet Union and the Eurozone, while the Chinese were in talks with the South-East Asian Trade Bloc about forming a super-trade bloc across the entire Asian continent. The International Banking Confederation had put forward a proposal to ban Bitcoins and the other cryptocurrencies it believed were destabilising the financial markets and its stranglehold on monetary policy.

Then there was the usual run of mergers and acquisitions between the big corporates and international conglomerates, which he skimmed over with a mix of boredom and anxiety, his eyes constantly flicking from the screen to the surrounding mall and up to the sky in search of Company soldiers and wasps.

He moved on to a more readable article about rock star Elman Ray, lead singer of the Mosquitoes, marrying Nancy Bloomer, daughter of Rickhardt Bloomer, the founder of Bloomer Corp – the nanotechnology company that had taken the world by storm with its health-bots that could be sent into the bloodstream to seek and destroy cancer cells and other potentially fatal diseases and viruses. A technology discovered too late, sadly, to save his mother. He tried to imagine her face as best he could remember it, before the worst of her disease had left her gaunt and vacuous. It was hard, but he found her for a second, before she drifted away.

He looked back at the article. It had photos of the wedding, and the many elite guests attending some grand castle overlooking the sea. Johnson tried to imagine what life would be like as an elite – private jets to travel the world, eating the most delicious dinners every night, living in a bubble beyond the everyday struggles of the common person. But as he looked at the photos of the wedding, the faces of the rich and famous didn't seem any happier than the faces of those in the café or the people walking along the mall. There was sadness in them all.

He turned off the tablet, put it back in his bag and finished the last of his coffee with a big swig. He scanned his wrist chip to pay his bill and then hurriedly left the café. He pulled his hat low and walked up the mall, looking for the street that led to the restaurant he had visited with Maya. More than a week had passed since then, and so much had happened. He was a bit unsure of himself and kept questioning whether he would be able to recognise it. Eventually, he came to a street that seemed vaguely familiar. It was right by an exit. *This must be it,* he thought, as he walked along the street. After a few hundred metres, he rounded a bend and saw the restaurant on the left-hand side. The gate was closed.

"Alfonzo, are you there?" he shouted.

There was no sound. He looked around and checked that no one was watching, then kicked open the gate. Johnson walked up to the restaurant's glass doors and peered inside.

He banged on the door. "Alfonzo," he yelled.

He heard a heavy door opening, then the sound of feet walking up stairs. He saw a head appear behind the bar and then a man coming towards him. It was Miguel, looking at him suspiciously. Miguel opened the door, just a little, and spoke through the gap: "What are you doing here?"

"Miguel, I am sorry to bother you," Johnson began, his voice soft, "but I am looking for Maya."

"She isn't here," Miguel replied.

"I know, but she is missing at work and I, ah, thought you might know where she is."

"Missing at work, at your work?" Miguel rubbed his moustache.

"Yes, that's right."

"What do you mean missing?"

"Well, I went to find her, and she wasn't in her department. And they say she never worked there, and they don't know who she is." Johnson spoke frantically. "I didn't know what to do... so I came here."

"Right." Miguel tapped one of his black shoes against the floor. "I cannot help you *now*," he said suddenly. "What is your name again?"

"Johnson."

"Ah, yes, Mr Johnson. Perhaps if you come back tonight. Yes? After we close up, Alfonzo will be here, and we can talk then."

"Alright, what time do you close?"

"Come just before midnight. It should be clear then."

"Okay, I'll see you later then." Johnson looked up at Miguel hopefully.

"Now I must go," Miguel said. He closed the door quickly, as if he were trying to keep out a strong breeze.

Johnson stood for a moment and then turned back towards the gate, walking slowly, pondering what they might say to him when he returned. He felt a chill run up his spine. He didn't know if he trusted Miguel, or if he should trust these two strangers at all, but it was his only real chance of finding her.

He walked back to the mall, wondering what the hell he was going to do with himself until midnight. It was there that he spotted two Gorilla Industries soldiers – in their unmistakable yellow-and-brown uniform and red face-scanner goggles. They were carrying heavy guns. He ducked around a corner, knowing they could easily pick up that he was an employee with a face scan; even just general crowd scanning could show him up as an employee unauthorised to be out of the compound. *I need to find a safe house,* he thought as he grabbed the Gorilla cap off his head and stuffed it in his bag.

4.

Johnson hurried up to the house as rain fell around him. He banged on the front door. A tall, elegant girl with long blonde hair answered.

"Hello," she said.

"Is Conrad in?" gasped Johnson.

"Conrad," she yelled out, "it's for you."

Conrad came bounding down the hallway. He was wearing a silky blue robe. "Jay, what are you doing here? Come in, come in," he beckoned. Johnson squeezed through the gap between the woman and the door. "This is Delilah," Conrad said, pointing to the woman.

"I'm going," Delilah said.

"Right, okay." Conrad shuffled on the spot. "You want to head in..." he said, nudging Johnson up the hallway.

"You need to fix me up," Delilah interrupted.

Conrad nodded. He turned to Johnson: "You okay? You look a bit harried."

Johnson stood open-mouthed, his arms hanging limply by his sides. "Not really, mate. I need your help."

"Okay. Go inside and make yourself comfortable. I'll be with you in a tick." Conrad winked and then turned back to Delilah, tapping her gently on the backside.

Johnson walked up the hallway, past three paintings. One had a green-and-pink pyramid on it; the next had a painting of a dark face and its exact opposite in light; and the last had a pile of clocks melting like cheese, with a train zooming into the horizon.

At the end of the hall was a large lounge with a low coffee table and three double couches that sat tightly in the room, hemming in the table like a pack of hungry jackals. The room was set up to face a large white wall, and Johnson could just make out the outline of the giant HV wall screen. He walked over and touched the wall gently, remembering those hours spent talking to Conrad over AppChat while watching the Chargers play football.

Johnson heard Conrad and Delilah whispering and then the door close. Conrad returned. He looked concerned. "Jay, what's going on, my good man?"

"Sorry, I didn't mean to disturb you with umm..." Johnson paused. "I didn't realise you had company."

"Nonsense. She was leaving anyway. Now why do I have the pleasure of your company?"

"It's a long story," Johnson said as he gazed at an elephant statue in the corner.

"Well, I'm listening. Just let me get some proper clothes on." Conrad darted out of the room. "Was it *the* girl?" he yelled from the other room.

Johnson snorted.

Conrad reappeared a few moments later wearing a pair of brown trousers and a green T-shirt. "Do you want a beer?" he asked.

"Yeah, alright," Johnson replied.

Conrad ducked back the way he came and then reappeared with two beers. He sat down on the couch facing the wall screen and put the beers on the two coasters that were sitting on the table. He leaned forward, his arms hanging between his legs;

the same pose Johnson had often seen when they watched the Chargers. "What happened? Why aren't you at work?"

"I left work."

"What do you mean? You left?"

Johnson took a swig of beer. He told Conrad about his attempts to find Maya.

"At least you went to find her, like I suggested." Conrad winked. "Otherwise, you'd still be waiting there for her to show up."

"I guess," Johnson replied half-heartedly. "Although now I don't have a job, so there's that."

Conrad sighed. "Faarrk... You went the whole hog. What happened?"

He explained about Rachael's betrayal and the termination warning. "And all the while they denied any knowledge of Maya," he added. "I just felt uneasy about what they were saying, and I didn't want to be there. And I wanted to find her, so I packed up my stuff and left."

Conrad listened, his chin resting on the back of his hand. "What a bunch of bastards."

Johnson went on: "I don't trust them. And I want to make sure she's alright..." he trailed off, wondering for a moment if this was all a ruse to avoid him. He went red and began to sweat. He mopped his brow and took another gulp of beer.

"Ah, I'm sure you'll find her," Conrad said, leaning forward and tapping him reassuringly on the knee.

Johnson remembered why he was there. He fidgeted on the couch and then asked his friend if he could stay. He explained that he was not going back to Gorilla Industries and didn't have anywhere else to go.

Conrad scratched at his neck. He sipped his beer, looking

slightly uncomfortable in the moment. "Are you sure that's wise mate?"

Johnson let out a deep sigh. "I don't have any family left, Conrad, and you're the only one I could come to." He felt his eyes getting hot.

"They don't know you're here, do they?" Conrad asked. "Gorilla Industries, I mean."

"No. I didn't tell them anything."

"Okay, okay, that's good," Conrad replied. He chuckled. "I'm not sure The Marketplace would want me housing a known work fugitive."

"It won't be for long. Just tonight and then I'll get going."

"It's fine, Jay. You can stay. It's a good thing that I get the whole weekend off, hey, so we can hang out tomorrow. I'll have to cancel my plans with Delilah, though." He smiled.

There was a loud knock at the door. Johnson froze. Could it be the Company soldiers already, come to drag him back to work? Surely, they didn't know he was here, he'd been so careful when he left. And he'd hardly done anything wrong. It didn't make sense, but he was frightened, nonetheless. He looked at Conrad, his eyes pleading for his friend to keep his cover.

Conrad stood up gingerly, a funny look on his face. He pursed his lips. "Who do you think that is?" he asked, his voice slightly higher pitched than normal. He sauntered slowly down the hallway to the door.

Johnson heard it open, his heart pounding.

He heard a jangle of something, then a female voice: "Sorry, I forgot my bracelet."

He heard Conrad's voice too – "Delilah, my dear. Are you back for more already?" – followed by a great gush of laughter.

5.

Una stood under an awning, sheltered from the storm. The rain lashed across in front of her at an angle, which meant it was likely to be natural rain from a natural storm that had washed through the city as she returned from the lake house. Darkness had descended and she could barely see a few yards in front.

She shivered as the wind beat across her. She flipped up the collar of her blue jacket and put her hands in the pockets.

He came out of the shadows, an umbrella over his head. He stood for a moment, as if checking it was her, and then rushed forward and stopped in front of her. "Maya... is that you?"

"Yeah, it's me," she replied. "We appreciate you coming." She was glad she had got him to come meet her out here, away from the compound, away from the danger it posed. "I didn't want to go back in," she added.

"And rightly so," he said. "It's better this way."

She nodded.

"I thought you were done at Gorilla Industries."

"I am. But I need to get Johnson out."

He stood under the awning, frowning. "Right," he said as he shook the water off his umbrella.

She wiped away some rain from her eye. "Where is he?" she asked. "I thought you were bringing him."

The man shook his head. "He's not there," he said. A flash of lightning cracked across the sky and illuminated him, showing a beige raincoat with the hood up, covering his grey hair. There were black circles around his tired-looking eyes. She felt sorry for him in that moment – for what they had put him through, what *she* had put him through.

"I looked everywhere," he added. "His computer was left on, with him logged in as if he was sitting at his desk… but he's gone."

"What about at his house? Did you check that?"

"I checked his home unit and it's empty."

"You went inside?" she probed.

"Yes. I walked around and couldn't find him. His Home Intelligence Unit was off too, and there were some clothes and things strewn across the bed… which makes me think he's gone."

"Are you sure?" she said. She began to fret, moving haphazardly around the little spot they had commandeered under a warehouse awning. Splashes of water hit her jacket and hair. "I need to find him."

The man held his hands up before her. "I know. And I was a bit worried about that, so I tracked his Eye-Tab."

She raised her eyebrows. "Okay, where is he?"

"The signal is coming from the port area. He's either gone out to sea, or it's broken, or…" He stopped.

"You don't think something has happened to him?" she asked, worry strewn across her face. She hoped for a second that he had escaped on a boat, left this god-forsaken city and headed off in search of a better life. But, almost immediately, the thought came over her that his body may have been dumped.

"I honestly think he flushed it down the toilet," said the man, almost smiling as if this gave him a strange pleasure. "It's tracking right near the sewer pipes, in the treatment bay area."

She breathed out heavily. "That's good," she said. "I'll need to find him another way." She began to move through the rain. She turned back to Melville. "How long until they work out he's gone?"

Melville opened his umbrella again and held it over his head. "I'll hold them off for as long as I can," he said.

"That will help," she replied as the water saturated her hair and face. "Thanks for your help, Melville. For everything you did for us."

"I didn't have a choice," said Melville quietly, almost to himself. He scratched angrily at his chin and said nothing further. Then, just before she turned the corner, he shouted out, "Is that it? Is my son safe now?"

"He always was," she replied as she disappeared into the night.

6.

Johnson arrived at the restaurant half an hour early. He had intended to wait outside until he was summoned, but the powerful force of Maya drove him inside. He walked through the gate. He looked up at the great willow tree looming over the courtyard, sensing its powerful, everlasting essence. The storm that had lashed the city had eased, leaving the leaves and everything glistening with water.

He headed inside the restaurant and sat at a small table in the corner. Despite the late hour, there were still some diners enjoying the last of their meals. One large group was sitting around a long wooden table. They were drinking wine and talking loudly. As Johnson sat awkwardly at his table, they broke into song. He hadn't heard the song before, but he liked it. They chanted the chorus like an old sea shanty: *"The Union forever, defending their rights."*

He was drawn to the way they sang - arms draped over one another, comfortable in their closeness. He almost wished they'd call him over, to take his mind off things, but they only glanced his way, and then fell-back into their wine and songs.

Heat beat down at him from a circular heat-cylinder above; he almost wanted to rip off his shirt. His leg tapped on the ground like a demented jazz drummer. He watched Miguel gliding between tables, picking up plates and balancing them carefully on his hands and arms. A young lady with a stout body and happy face was helping wait the tables. She rushed around the restaurant at an unrelenting speed.

Johnson kept looking up at Miguel whenever he passed his table, but he seemed unable or unwilling to acknowledge his presence. He wished Miguel would look at him or nod his way – anything to acknowledge his presence. Instead, Miguel continued to ignore him, while Johnson grew more and more agitated.

The waiting became taxing. Johnson began to play with a candle in the middle of the table. He slid his finger into the melting wax, feeling a hint of pain, and then, just before his finger burnt, he pulled it out with a rush of adrenaline, watching as the wax solidified around his fingertip.

He felt a presence near him and glanced up. Miguel winked as he brushed past. Johnson smiled and started to relax a little – they knew he was here.

He waited another 15 minutes, until the last few customers had dribbled out, and then got up with his bag and walked over to the bar. Miguel was standing behind it, cleaning a wineglass.

"Ah, yes. You are here," Miguel said as he put down the glass and dried his hands.

"Wait there, please." Miguel turned around, opened a hatch in the floor and walked down some stairs. He returned after a couple of minutes. "Quickly," he said. "Let's go."

Johnson followed Miguel down into a cellar. It was dimly lit, with a wooden floor and a low concrete roof. The room was filled with boxes of canned food and other restaurant supplies. It smelled of soggy cardboard.

They slowly weaved through the maze of boxes until they reached the other side of the cellar. At the end was a wall of boxes that reached the dank ceiling, with words like 'Beaujolais

Nouveau' and 'La Rioja Tinto' printed on the front.

Miguel began dismantling a stack of boxes, one at a time, pulling them down from the top with surprising strength and speed. As the stack dwindled, a hidden door was revealed. Miguel opened the door and ushered Johnson through. It was low, and he had to duck down to get into the adjoining room.

The room was small and smelled of mould. There was a light bulb in the middle of the ceiling, giving off a bright-yellow light. On one side was a couch covered in red and yellow pillows and a coarse woollen blanket. Johnson looked around and spotted Alfonzo in the corner, hunched over a desk strewn with papers, cans of drink and a battered old laptop.

Alfonzo got up from his desk, walked over to Johnson and shook his hand. "Sit down, sit down," he said. Johnson nodded and sat down on the old office chair beside the desk, dropping his bag down next to him. Alfonzo sat opposite him.

"I am sorry to disturb you both," Johnson began, moving his eyes between the two men, "but I needed to come and see you."

"Why is that?" Alfonzo asked.

"Maya!"

"Yes, Miguel mentioned you had information about, hmm, Maya."

"She is missing," Johnson said, feeling the pain of the words.

Alfonzo looked intently at Johnson. "Missing, you say."

"Yeah, and I need to find her."

"And you came to us?"

"Well, you both know her, and you were so welcoming to us that night we came for dinner, I thought you may have been friends."

"We are friends, this is true," Alfonzo replied.

Johnson leaned forward in his chair. "Right. So maybe you could help me find her."

Alfonzo nodded. "Tell me, what happened to her?"

"We work together, or worked together, I should say, for a few weeks–"

"At Gorilla Industries, yes?"

"Yeah, that's right." Johnson replied, his confidence growing. "We had this amazing night together, and it doesn't really matter about that now, but we were going to see each other again. And then, well, I couldn't find her at work."

Alfonzo cleared his throat.

Johnson paused, and then went on: "And now they don't know who she is. They say she never worked there. But I know she does, because I met her there in the cafeteria."

"They are lying?"

"Yes," cried Johnson, almost jumping out of his seat. "This man – Raymond Melville, a manager from Human Resources – told me that she had never worked at Gorilla Industries. But I saw them together."

Alfonzo sat back in his chair. He was quiet for a moment. "Right. What department do you work in?"

"The Information Editing Unit," Johnson replied, his voice shaking. "It doesn't really matter."

"And her?"

"It is not important."

"Perhaps it is?" Alfonzo said as he twirled his bushy beard.

Johnson peered into Alfonzo's heavy eyes. He could see the man was listening to his words carefully. Johnson slowed himself down and explained in minute detail his efforts to track down

Maya, his trip to the Research Laboratory, and their stringent denial of her existence.

Alfonzo wanted to know when he had last seen her.

"The day after we came here," Johnson said, remembering again that special day at the Botanical Gardens and the Millennium Museum. He went quiet. He thought he sensed growing concern on Alfonzo's face.

"When was that?"

"About a week ago," Johnson answered, slumping forward in his seat, feeling exhausted from the emotional toll of the day.

"This is concerning," Alfonzo said.

Miguel chimed in: "Something may have happened to her."

Johnson turned his head to face Miguel. It was the first time Miguel had spoken since they arrived in the underground office. He stood by the door like a sentry dog programmed for guard duty. "Momento," he said, before he turned and left the tiny underground office.

"Where is he going?" Johnson asked.

"He'll be back," replied Alfonzo. "He's just going to check in with some of Una's, ah, friends."

"Who's Una?"

"Maya, I meant Maya," Alfonzo answered quickly. "But sometimes she calls herself Una too."

"Really? What do you mean?" asked Johnson. "

"Don't worry. She is a girl of many names. And these are just two." Alfonzo smiled, flecks of white teeth gleaming through his black beard.

Johnson wondered why Maya had not mentioned any of this. He must have look bemused, because Alfonzo took a deep breath and began to explain: "She used to work for a group of people who are trying to fight against this system. And maybe that's why she changes her name all the time – in case they had her on a database somewhere and wouldn't give her the job, or they wanted to charge her with some bullshit offence."

"Maybe they found out about that," Johnson offered, "and that's why she's missing."

"Perhaps you are right," said Alfonzo, "perhaps you are right."

The door swung open and Miguel walked back in.

The pair convened in the middle of the room and started talking in a language Johnson didn't understand. After a few minutes of heated conversation, Alfonzo nodded and turned back to Johnson. "Will you help us find her, Johnson?"

"Of course," he replied.

"Are you sure you want to do this" Alfonzo said, a warm sadness emanating from his being as if he had just caught a vision of his younger self playing carelessly in a park.

Johnson stood up again, a rush of energy pulsed through him. "What? Of course! I'll do anything," he said with breathless enthusiasm, his hands clasped together, his legs trembling.

"No, there's nothing we can do at this moment. But stay here tonight. You can sleep there." Alfonzo pointed to the couch in the back corner of the room.

Johnson stood, unmoved, quietly accepting the proposal.

"Okay, we'll leave first thing tomorrow," Alfonzo stated firmly. "Get some sleep."

Miguel and Alfonzo marched out of the room and slammed the door shut. Johnson looked over at the mouldy, wine-stained couch in the corner and sighed. He wanted to go now and find Maya – it was burning at him – but he had to wait. And the waiting scared him most of all.

7.

Johnson tossed and turned on the lumpy couch, unable and unwilling to sleep without the help of his trusty Dream Weaver. His mind raced with endless thoughts that seemed to be on a constant loop and wouldn't let up, filling him with anxiety that bubbled over into spasms and jolts. He closed his eyes more tightly, desperate for a wink of sleep, for the time to pass, for morning to come.

Eventually, he drifted off into a restless but natural slumber...

He is standing in a wooden house. He feels calm. He walks, almost floating, through the open kitchen area. He passes a bench-top scattered with breadcrumbs. He should wipe that up, he thinks, but leaves it and moves on through the house. He is drawn outside, through the low purple archway, which he must duck under, into the laundry and then out through the flyscreen door, which clatters behind him. He feels cold stone underfoot. He finds his sandals by the door and slips them on each foot, stumbling forward as he tries to put the right one on.

Clothes are drying on the makeshift clothesline – a few of his, but mostly hers. They are colourful, loose-fitting shirts and pants – oranges, blues, olive and earthy greens, some deep red like blood. He should wear more colour, he thinks, as he looks down at his black jeans and faded, nothing shirt.

On his left is a wooden garden plot. It was once a set of shelves or a cupboard, but now, hollowed out, on its side and filled with dirt, it makes a fine herb garden, replete with rosemary and thyme and coriander. There are some new seeds too – ones they recently planted together.

He walks over with the hose and slowly fills a metal watering-can to the top. He pours the water gently over the soil, excited by the prospect of those seeds turning into seedlings and then swathes of rocket, mint and parsley.

He knows they will grow. He doesn't know how he knows. He just knows, as if he's been planting them for years. Plus, any food that he can grow means less food they need to buy, less they will want for in the future.

He walks over to the bigger garden. It runs all the way down the wooden fence. Some of it is falling apart, but it doesn't matter. The neighbours are like them... and their food will be shared.

He wanders carefully through the garden, his feet stepping gingerly from rock to rock. It is lush and green and full of life, with vibrant leaves spurting forth and reaching for the sun. The zucchini plant is taking over. He reaches down and plucks off a solitary zucchini from under the leaves. It needs a bit more growth, he muses, as he examines the fleshy vegetable. He takes a bite. No point wasting it.

There is a strawberry patch and some ginger. By the fence are tomato vines, and then up further are the carrots, lettuce and broccoli; between them all are yellow and white flowers – little natural fences of majestic beauty and colour. The potatoes wind their way through the ground in front of him. They are still small, but he hopes they will grow bigger. He should put some fertiliser on them, he thinks, as he walks past the lemon and mandarin trees. On his left is the chicken coop, made from wood and bits of old fence strapped together haphazardly with wire. Three chickens walk around, pecking at last night's leftovers, eating the remnants of peeled beetroot, and scraps of lettuce and tomato.

"Tea," whispers someone behind him.

He turns around. She is standing there, a green scarf holding back her long, dark, curly hair. It has grown a lot and hangs over her shoulders. He walks towards her. She has two mugs of tea in her hands – splotchy brown, uneven mugs that she made with her bare hands. She gives one over, smiling.

"Thanks, Maya," he says.

"Anything for my handsome man."

He laughs at that. She knows how to make him feel good.

"How are the potatoes going?" she asks.

"I was just going to put some juice from the worm farm on them," he says.

"It's great, isn't it," she says as she looks admiringly around the garden and then carefully sips her tea.

He follows suit. "Yeah, and we made it together," he says with a grin. He pulls her towards him and kisses her clumsily on the cheek.

"Ah, careful," she says as she steadies the tea in her hand. Some of it drops onto the pavers below, leaving little wet, fleeting splotches.

"We did it for him," she says as she looks down at her belly and rubs the little bump that protrudes through her tight-fitting green T-shirt.

8.

She walked towards the station, her head down, her red hat low, covering her eyes. The early morning air felt crisp against her skin. On reaching the entrance, she rushed down the escalator, into the warm belly of the underground.

She hopped aboard a north-west train, which headed out from under the city to its limits, where order gave way to chaos. There was a frenetic energy to her every move, as if for the first time in a long time she didn't quite know who she was or what she was doing.

She took a seat on the train, fidgeting this way and that, her eyes avoiding the surveillance cameras.

She couldn't believe Johnson had left. Where had he gone? Was he coming back? Was it because of her? These questions had been racing through her mind since her meeting with Melville. He had helped her, of course, but he couldn't hold Gorilla Industries off forever, especially if they found out Johnson had gone. And then there was Lenmar and the humanists. She had to get him to them, but she didn't want to – who knew what they would do with him once he had served his purpose. Guilt racked her. What had she become?

She took out her PID and started writing a message:

Johnson. It is Maya. We need to talk. There is so much I have to tell you. It is urgent. Meet me at the Emerald Café, on the Winding Way, in the slums – head north-west beyond the city limits. Get the train to JP Morgan Station, then head halfway up the hill, past the markets. There's a four-leaf clover on the door. I'll be there soon. Your friend Eileen will be there. She will help us. I'm sorry for the trouble I've got you into. Love Maya.

It was risky using traceable channels like AppChat, but hers was a secure line and she had to try to save him. It was *her* fault that he was in this situation. His was one life she could actually affect *now*, not in some better, far-off future for which she had always pushed.

Her leg tapped incessantly on the train floor. She looked out the window as the train pulled into another station. It was one stop before the right one. She stood up, put her PID back in her shoulder bag and made her way to the exit. It was better from this station – further but safer. In case they were monitoring her messages.

She got off the train and traipsed along the main arteries of the slum. It was a long walk, maybe an hour, and she powered on, barely bothering to register the broken streets and tenements around her.

She made her way from the top, down the Winding Way, following a path through the ramshackle tenements of a forgotten part of the city. Her eyes peeled until she reached the Emerald Café. She went inside.

Eileen was behind the bar area. She looked up as Una walked in.

"Hi," said Eileen.

"Hey, ah, Eileen. Do you remember me?" Una asked. "I came here about a month ago. For Lenmar."

"Ah, yes," replied Eileen. "I remember. How did you get on at Gorilla Industries?"

"Fine, I guess."

"Get what you need?"

Una looked away and nodded.

"Did you come across my old friend, Johnson?" Eileen asked. "The one I told you about."

"Well, yes," Una replied. "That's what I'm here for, actually."

"He is still there. Wow!" Eileen exclaimed. She held up a mug and offered Una a tea.

"Yeah okay, thanks, but first, I really need your help."

"How is he?" Eileen asked. "Johnson, I mean."

"Not good. That's why I need your help. Well, Johnson needs your help."

"Sure. What can I do?" Eileen placed the mug down on the bar. Her green eyes followed Una carefully; the tension rising in the air between them.

"I need to get him out," Una replied. "He's in danger, from Gorilla Industries, from everyone."

"They… I mean, we used him for his security codes…" Una's eyes stayed on the floor, but she could feel Eileen's pressing in on her. "But I want to get him out, before they find out."

Eileen swore, and then muttered angrily about them being a bunch of heartless ideologues. "I told you not to use him," she said, as she stood up and moved around the bar, coming face to face with Una. "I gave you that information to help out; in the hope we could get access to the Gorilla Information Network. Not so you could fuck with my friend."

"I know, and I am so sorry," Una replied sadly. She met Eileen's furious gaze. "I didn't mean to… It just happened that way," she pleaded. There was silence for a moment before Una went on hurriedly, her hands a hive of movement: "It wasn't my choice.

Melville chose him, and then it was too late, and I had to just go along with it. And now I want to fix it."

"And how do you propose to do that?"

"I want to get him here. Get him away from any danger."

"And take him where? Back to Lenmar and your lot?"

"No, I'm not going back there, not with Johnson."

"But how can I trust you, after last time?" Eileen said, eyeing Una suspiciously. "After I helped you out, helped you get inside and find Melville. And then you went and took an innocent man – one I told you specifically to leave alone – and you turned him into another pawn in your games." Eileen held out her arms. "What the fuck are we fighting for?

Una put her head in her hands. "But you can trust me," she said, almost crying. "I like Johnson. And I want to help him. We connected, you know, and I want–"

Eileen began to cackle. "You want what? Johnson? Ha!" She laughed some more and then started coughing violently like an old smoker.

Una put her hands gently on Eileen's back, helping her stand back up again. "Maybe I just want to protect him, to help a person who is in danger," she said. "That's why I joined this group... why I became a humanist in the first place."

"You feel guilty, don't you?" said Eileen, tapping Una on the arm. "I know about that. I am Irish, and we have the guilt too." She rested one arm on the bar behind her. "He's a good man, a blameless one, and he doesn't deserve any of this."

"I know, I know," Una began, "and that's why I want to save him. He is what is worth fighting for. People like him deserve better. They could have been so much more than what they are now if they weren't slaves to a system that doesn't give a shit about any of them."

"You're damn right," said Eileen. "And that's why I helped you, why I always help."

"I know," said Una.

"Bring him back here then," Eileen demanded. "And I'll take care of it, but you have to leave him with me. I know some people he can hide out with here in the slums... at least while we work out a more secure plan."

"Thanks, Eileen, I'll make sure he gets here," said Una. "I'm so sorry–"

"Don't mention it again," replied Eileen. "You are trying to fix it now. And that's what matters."

9.

He was unsure if he was awake or asleep. He'd been in the same state for much of the night, huddled on the couch, his eyes closed, flashes of dreams interrupted by a rumbling anxiety that nagged at him like a shopkeeper at a market stall desperate for a sale.

There were no windows, so he couldn't tell if it was morning. He had no idea of the time. His tablet had run out of power. As he searched his bag for the charger, he wondered if he was trapped, held captive by Alfonzo and Miguel – two deranged fugitives keeping him locked in their basement forever.

When he did charge his device, he was relieved to see it was only 08:30. This realisation pacified the worst of his fears, and he lay down again and tried to get some more sleep, grabbing at it hopelessly like a toddler trying to catch a ball. He couldn't get comfortable and kept thinking about Maya – where was she being held, and why? A million possibilities crept into his fragile mind.

He started to get a pain in his head. It pulsated in his temple. He sweated. At first he thought it was the stale air, or the acute stress of the situation, but then he began to shake in violent, uncontrolled waves. He wondered if he was getting sick – a virus or superbug. But then it dawned on him, as he looked at his shaking hands, he may be suffering withdrawal symptoms from the concoction of Company pills he took each day. He grabbed hold of his duffel bag and rummaged around until he found a Pep-Me-Up pill. He took two. After a few minutes, the shakes began to subside and his headache lifted; but now he was nervous and fidgety, and he paced up and down the cramped, mouldy room, thinking only about Maya.

He grabbed his tablet and tried to log onto to the internet, to see if Maya had contacted him – she had his details after all – but there was no wi-fi, and no way to connect.

The cellar door suddenly flew open. Johnson jumped back as Miguel rushed in. “Come on, let’s go,” he said. “It’s time.”

“Shall I bring my bag?” Johnson asked.

Miguel nodded. Johnson grabbed his bag and followed Miguel through the cellar and back up the stairs to the restaurant.

Alfonzo was in the kitchen. “Ah, Johnson. How was your sleep?”

“Fine,” Johnson lied.

Alfonzo trotted over with a plate of food. He greeted Johnson with a jovial slap on the shoulder, and then handed him the plate with a toasted egg sandwich. “For you,” he said.

“Thanks, but I’m really not hungry,” Johnson said.

“You must eat,” Alfonzo retorted. “You have a long day ahead.”

Johnson took a bite. He felt the butter, egg and tomato salsa squelching in his mouth. He thanked Alfonzo, his mouth still full of food, then took another heavy bite. It was good, and it reminded him of his hunger. He rushed it down, eager to fill his stomach and to get on with things.

After he had eaten, Johnson held up his tablet. “Is there an internet connection I can use?” he asked.

Miguel shook his head. “There’s no time,” he said. “We need to get going.” And then the two men led Johnson out of the restaurant and through the garden. He looked up at the willow tree. It held an ancient beauty in its boughs. He wondered how many years it had seen. How many people had it silently watched? What was the world like when it had sprouted from a tiny seed?

Johnson tried to make small talk as they left the restaurant behind. He asked them about running it, but they didn't talk much. Johnson went quiet, his mind taking him back to last night's dream: the old house, the garden and the vegetable patch, Maya with her mugs of tea, and the coming of a child... his child. The idea excited him, madly almost, and he thought of his mother and what she would have said; how happy it would have made her.

"This way," Alfonzo called as Johnson veered off the wrong way.

"Where are we going?" Johnson asked.

"You'll see," was the only reply.

Johnson walked half a step behind the other two as they weaved through the backstreets of the city. Occasionally they passed the odd person walking their dog or heading to work. The buildings themselves were older than those in the business district, a mix of terraces and townhouses running along the crumbling streets of a city in decay. Johnson thought of the hotel where he and Maya had spent the night together.

They stopped at a garage. Out the front was an old man with dark skin and sunglasses, sitting on a plastic crate. He smoked a cigar and stared off into the distance.

Alfonzo walked up to the man, bent down and said something quietly in his ear. The man seemed to wake from his trance. He looked at Johnson, then got off his crate and knocked against the metal garage door.

The garage door opened with a creak, revealing a white van.

A heavy-set young man with blond hair and a big nose bounced out of the vehicle. He walked over to them. "Is this him?" he said.

Miguel nodded.

"We need you to give us your devices," said the heavy-set fellow as he took Johnson's bag. He threw it to the old man, who took it over to the van and began looking through it. "And we will have to blindfold you," he added. He spoke in short halting waves.

"What do you mean?" Johnson replied.

"They won't take you without a blindfold," Alfonzo said. "As I said, these people you are seeing... let me say, they are protective of their privacy."

"Here." the heavy-set man handed Johnson a blindfold. "You can tie it yourself."

Johnson sighed and reluctantly tied it around his head, covering his eyes. The blindfold was wrenched tighter, painfully so. Everything was black. He couldn't see a thing. An arm was on him, pulling him forward.

"It will be alright," Alfonzo said. "But we have to go back to the restaurant."

"You're going?" Johnson stammered, barely believing what he was hearing. He felt Alfonzo's thick arm on his shoulder. "They will take you on to find Maya," Alfonzo said, his arm squeezing into Johnson, "and when you find her, come back and we will celebrate with a great fiesta."

"We will take him to them now," said the heavy-set man. He seemed in a hurry.

"Thanks," said Alfonzo. "Good luck! And you too, Johnson."

Johnson heard a grunt from Miguel and then the sounds of disappearing feet.

He heard a door slide open. He was pushed down into a seat,

and a belt was wrapped across his shoulder.

"Shall I secure him?" he heard a voice say.

"No. Let's sort it once we're on the road."

Then he heard the two men get inside the van, one in the front and one in the seat beside him. The engine started. They were driving. Johnson sat quietly, listening for any sounds that would help him work out his location. He asked them a few times where they were taking him, but his questions were met with silence. He was in complete darkness. And scared – scared of where he was being taken, to whom, and with a nagging thought that they might just pull the van over and shoot him there and then.

His worry intensified when the man next to him said, "I'll do it now." He thought he heard a bottle being opened. Then he smelled something – a metallic, chemical smell. It was right under his nose. He pulled his head back hard against the headrest, recoiling from whatever it was. "What's that?" he shouted at whoever would listen, his arms scrabbling about in front of him. Then his head began to spin, dizziness overtook him... then nothing.

He could smell a strange, awful odour, like rotten eggs. It reeked, right into his nose. Everything was dark. He could feel the blindfold still on his face, cutting out the light. He had a headache and felt nauseous. He wanted to throw up, wanted to cough up everything, but nothing came. He couldn't do anything. His arms were lifeless, his throat could barely swallow. He drifted once more...

He was sitting on something soft, a sofa maybe. He could hear the noises of people coming and going, and voices. At first they were blurry sounds, but as time went by, the voices became clearer, forming into words. There was something about a park and some cameras and everything being ready. *Where am I?* he thought, wondering for a moment if he was dead and all this was some strange, dark waiting land...

The blindfold was taken off. Standing before him was a stocky woman. Everything else was fuzzy. He rubbed his eyes. The woman was in her 60s, with long grey hair. She had a kind-looking face and smiled reassuringly at Johnson. She was standing beside a massive bookshelf that ran the length of the wall. Johnson had never seen so many books. He was seated in a big, open room. It seemed to have separate adjoining rooms and various nooks and crannies. Johnson was in the largest area, which was surrounded by couches and what looked like filmmaking equipment. Everything was made of wood, and there was a sense of age to the place, a weathered history in the walls and floor.

"Would you like a drink?" the lady asked, pointing to a table with some glasses and a bottle of whiskey.

"No, it's fine," said Johnson. His voice was coarse. "Maybe some water?"

"Sure." The friendly-looking lady left the room. She returned with a glass of water. A much younger woman trailed behind her. She was thin, with long, slender arms, dark-brown skin and a full nose holding up thin silver glasses. She spoke hurriedly, exposing a gap in her front teeth: "You are Johnson, Information Editor at Gorilla Industries?"

Johnson felt as if her eyes were burrowing into his skull. "I was," he began, but then stopped, unsure what else to say. "Where am I?" he asked the grey-haired lady. His mind was cloudy and he couldn't remember how he had got there.

"You are with us," she replied, a smile on her face, "and you are in good hands."

The younger woman leaned forward. "We are a group of underground activists trying to make this a fairer and more just system."

"This is Parks," said the lady, pointing to the girl. "They call me Auntie Norma. And over there is Camus." She pointed to a man sitting in the shadows in one of the room's little nooks. He was dark-featured, with a hook-nose, heavy jowls and thick, pushed-back hair, and was seated at a white desk covered with screens and digital devices.

Johnson looked at Parks dressed tightly in black, her clothes in stark contrast to Auntie Norma's loose-fitting white robes. *Where is Maya?* he wondered.

"We appreciate what you have done," Auntie Norma began, moving slowly around in front of Johnson, "coming here to help us like this."

"So we can access the Gorilla Information Network," said Camus from his seat in the corner, "and correct some of the misinformation that is being put out in the name of our global neo-liberalist system."

Right now Johnson didn't care about the neo-liberalist system; he didn't even know what it was. He took a deep breath through his nose, smelling again the strange stink that seemed to pervade the air. "Can you help me find Maya?" he asked in a slow, soft drawl.

"Ahhh, Una..." Parks said with a hint of sadness. "We haven't found her."

"But you will, right?" Johnson pressed, as he rubbed his temple, which was still throbbing; a deep pain right in his brain.

"We are working on it," Camus replied. "But we need some

time to hack in and try to locate her. Then we will see."

"See what?" Johnson said.

The three strangers looked at one another ominously.

Johnson's mind seemed to sharpen. He started to piece together how he had arrived. Images of the last day flooded in. *Where is Alfonzo?* Then he remembered the van and the two men, then nothing... *I must have blacked out,* he thought, *or been drugged.* His eyes began to search the room for the two men who'd brought him here.

Camus got up from his desk, walked over to Auntie Norma and whispered something in her ear. He turned to Johnson. "I have to go," he said. "We salute you," he added as he left the room.

Johnson stood up, looking nervously across the room, and then walked over to Parks and Auntie Norma. "Those two men who brought me here–" he began, but Auntie Norma cut him off, her hand raised as if in muted apology.

"They are gone," she said. "They delivered you to us – that's all that matters."

He nodded, and scratched at his head. "What is it that you do here?" he asked. His eyes fell to the floor. "This group I mean."

"We fight for justice," Parks replied sharply, "for people like you."

A man strode into the room. There was great purpose in his stride, in his being. He was strong-featured with a trim layer of brown stubble over his chin and cheeks. On his head he wore a black beret with a little symbol in the middle. Underneath were two piercing blue eyes that shone like moonstones.

"You worked for one of the big four information providers, right?" said the man, not waiting for Johnson's answer before he went on. "And you know what it is like working for these huge companies." He came to a stop next to Johnson and looked him straight in the eyes. "They are enslaving their workers. Workers like you." He paused. "For what? To make more money for themselves. Worse still, no one cares to stop it. People are worthless now, like chickens in a battery farm; objects to be used up and then discarded in the constant search of profits... profits for the already rich; for the greedy selfish elites who control this world. And it's only getting worse."

"We need to rise up," Parks added.

The words triggered a memory - the words of the Renegade. *It must be him*. The voice, the beret, and the piercing eyes that burnt with fierce passion as he spoke - this was the man he'd been told to dread, the man who had inspired him with his 'rise up' film, the one he'd blocked from the server. He was saying the same things now as he'd said over the screen. "Are you anti-globalists?" Johnson blurted out, unsure how far he should go, yet unable to control himself.

Parks shook her head violently and turned away.

"That is something they call us," said the man carefully, "but we are not anti-globalists. We see the failures of globalisation, the way it has destroyed communities and cultures, but it is not our creed. We are humanists. We fight for people. We put people over profit, workers over robots, community over corporations. That is what we're about - the greater good. We are humanists, not anti-globalists."

Parks interrupted: "They call us anti-globalists. They say we blow things up, but they speak lies. All lies." There was furious anger in her voice. "They want people to hate us, to see us as the enemy, when the enemy is the system that keeps the people enslaved. Divide and conquer, it's always their way."

"And we want to change that system," said the man as he adjusted his beret.

Johnson lost his balance a little, overwhelmed by what he was hearing. He steadied himself, a sense of calm rising up through him. "Are you the Renegade?" he asked.

"You know of him?" The man had a sly grin on his face.

"Yeah, I saw him in an online-vid. He was holding up an anti-globalist flag," said Johnson, his eyes locked onto the same symbol – the crushing boot – that adorned the man's beret.

"That was a humanist flag," said the man, "the collective of people fighting against rampant, unregulated capitalism."

"Was that you?"

The Renegade nodded. "If you have seen that footage, then you already know."

Johnson couldn't believe it. He was in the same room as the Renegade – the man who had told him and the world to rise up. And now they were talking face to face. He shifted uncomfortably in his seat, unsure what to say.

"Was Maya an anti-globalist? Johnson asked tentatively. "I mean humanist," he clarified.

"She was a part of our group, yes," said the Renegade. "We work together on certain projects, but she isn't always here with us. We are a disparate group that works from different places, different cells."

"We are part of everything, inside everyone," said Parks.

"As Parks said, we are more than any individual," added the Renegade.

"So then you know where Maya is?"

"We think," said the Renegade, "that she is at Gorilla Industries."

9.

"She not there," said Johnson, who began to frantically explain his attempts to find her.

The Renegade interrupted him: "Listen, we know your story, Johnson, but she went back to find you."

Johnson stared open-mouth at the Renegade. Afraid for Maya, but there was also a buzz of excitement in the knowledge that she had gone to search him out.

"We don't know exactly what happened," the Renegade added. "She came here to help us with our mission, but then she went back to Gorilla Industries to find you. And we haven't seen her since. And that's why we need you." The Renegade pointed his index finger at Johnson. "We need your help to find her."

"How? How can I help?" Johnson stammered.

"We need you to get us in, using your access as an Information Editor. Camus, our computer whiz, can log in to Gorilla Industries and look through her personnel logs, find out her last logins. And if that doesn't show up anything, then we can go through their security footage and see if we can find out what happened..."

"Security will have her! At the security dome!" exclaimed Johnson, remembering the daunting image of hundreds of Company soldiers marching in lines to the beat of a drum. "Do they know who she is? That she is one of you, a humanist, I mean?"

"We are not sure about that, but we need to find out, and we need your help. Only you can bypass the online security so we can log on to their systems."

He shuddered. *What am I getting into?* he wondered as his eyes flicked between the three humanists surrounding him.

"She needs your help, Johnson," said Auntie Norma softly. "We all do."

"Okay, I guess I have to," Johnson said, his voice cracking

slightly under the strain of his decision. "I have nowhere to go, and I want to help find her."

"Thanks, Johnson. We appreciate your help," said the Renegade. "You are one of us now – a true humanist." And with that he was gone, returning the same way he had come, his last words still lingering behind him.

The room went quiet. No one said anything. A bird squawked somewhere outside, breaking the silence that enveloped them all. "She is my friend too," said Parks after a few moments. "I'm glad you are helping us."

"I just hope she is okay," said Johnson, "and... we are not too late."

"She knew what she was doing," said Parks. "She made her own choices, like we do every day, as we must to continue this fight. But it was always her choice, and that is the key. She wasn't forced into it by a company or the elites using the threat of a life in the slums without food or shelter to get her to do their dirty work and make them wealthier. I know her well – she is my friend – and she would want us to finish the mission first. That would be her priority... and then we can look for her."

Johnson was unsure what she was talking about. "What mission? Shouldn't we be helping Maya?"

"Yes, of course," said Auntie Norma. "But we only have one chance with this. I'll get Camus to explain it properly when he gets back. We can only get access once with the live DNA scan, and we need to use that to find Maya, of course – which we should do as her friends – but also, we have an opportunity to get some other content up online." She walked over to the couch and sat down. "Two birds with one stone, and you are that stone, Johnson," she added with a cackle.

9.

"Are they the Renegade's films?" Johnson asked, as he sat down beside Auntie Norma; a strange, almost unwanted exhilaration welling up inside him, mixed with a deep-seated fear in the pit of his stomach.

"Yes, them of course, but others too: we have an important exposé of this whole system, which simply must come out. It is probably the most important thing we've ever done..." she trailed off.

"We are going to expose the Government retirement homes for what they are," Parks added forcefully.

The retirement homes! My father! Johnson couldn't believe it. He opened his mouth, ready to speak about his father, but then stopped as the words reached his lips.

"But first we have to remove your wrist chip," said Parks, moving in front of where he sat.

"My wrist chip?" Johnson asked, looking confused.

Parks nodded. "We will have to remove it now."

Johnson looked down at his arm where it was inserted. "But why?"

"They can track it."

His body jolted. "Are they tracking me now?"

"No. The chip was scrambled before you came here, but that scrambling can be undone. And if the authorities are looking for you, they will get it working again eventually, and then locate you on the Maps system. There will be police and security drones swarming this place. And then our efforts will be over. So, as you can see, we need to remove it and remove it now."

Johnson looked down at his wrist. He felt the skin. The small, hard chip was underneath, as always. He had never considered that a humble wrist chip could be used to track people. It made sense, though – everyone was chipped to make it easier to buy things and pay for services, but it also meant everyone could be tracked, their movements followed on a map.

"How would I get around without it, on the car-grid, or if I needed to buy things?" he asked.

"You don't need it," Auntie Norma answered. "We make dummy chips that we can use as a replacement. They are just as good as the real thing, but are untraceable. We can use them for a week or so. Then we toss them and use a new one. That way, no one knows where we are and what we're doing. They can't use the car-grid to control our movements, or digital money to stop us from buying our supplies – which are two of their main weapons in squashing rebellion."

Auntie Norma walked over to the table and poured herself a shot of whiskey. She poured two more and handed them to Parks and Johnson. Johnson took a sip. He winced. He remembered his father downing bottle after bottle of the stuff in those months they had lived together, before he went into the home. He felt the skin where the wrist chip sat, knowing that by removing it, he was also removing his last connection to the real world – but was it real?

Auntie Norma continued: "That is why they got rid of money in the first place. Without money, everyone is on a chip or a card, and those chips and cards can be blocked, and then people can be cut off from food, goods and transport. It was a smart move by governments that have become more and more authoritarian with the advent of new technologies."

Parks chimed in: "It is corporate fascism: keeping the people in servitude, beholden to companies, under the whims of the State."

Auntie Norma agreed. "It is a great power they wield. And

they say they do it all to protect us." She snorted. "From what, I'll never know."

"Okay, get rid of it," said Johnson suddenly. "I don't want it." He extended his arm and rolled up the sleeve of his shirt. Parks felt the chip under his skin. "I'll get a knife," she said. She walked out of the room and into the kitchen area.

He looked over at Auntie Norma. "Will it hurt?" he asked.

"Only a little. They don't put them in very deep."

Parks returned to the room with a knife. It looked sharp. Johnson's eyes widened. He shuddered. He watched as she made her way towards him.

"To no more wrist chip," Auntie Norma said as she raised her glass.

Johnson gulped down the rest of his whiskey. He closed his eyes, unable to watch. He imagined the knife slicing his wrist, and then unbearable pain. He waited for the cold metal of the blade.

"To being a person, not a product," Parks said as she cut into his skin.

10.

Una walked down the hill, away from Eileen and the Emerald Café. Her eyes blinked in the light, adjusting from the darkness of the little café. She burped up some tea. There was only so much she could drink. She needed time to think, away from Eileen and the café, so she walked along, looking here and there at the broken-down buildings of the slum, hoping against hope to see Johnson on her way.

She had her PID with her and intended on sending him another message - give him the directions again. He hadn't responded all day to her last one. There had been radio silence, and this worried her. They could have traced her message, they could have traced Johnson, and then who knows what would have happened to him.

She reached a small park, no bigger than a house, with a rusty swing set sitting motionless by an overgrown garden. She watched a child run up to it. "Mummy, can I go on the swing?"

His mum was right behind him, and she plopped him on the swing. Una could hear the joints squeaking a little with the movement. The boy cried with excitement, "Higher, Mummy, higher."

She saw an armed hornet drone fly overhead, loaded up heavily like an overweight pig. It contrasted against the boy on the swing, loving his moment of freedom and adrenalin. She watched him again, before a flash lit up the sky. She heard a huge explosion rock through the earth and air. It filled her with dread and she turned her attention back up the hill to where the noise had come from, from where she had wandered.

She left the park behind and quickly headed back the way she had come. There was a heavy energy in the air, a commotion of people who seemed to be walking haphazardly in all directions. There was sound, so much sound – yells and screams and clattering. She never knew the slums could be this noisy. Smoke and dust swirled around her.

As she got closer to the Emerald Café, she could hear shouting and see smoke rising. Dark engulfing clouds billowed upwards. There was heat in the air, flames leapt into the sky and she was surrounded by screams – dreadful screams. The din grew louder. Hornets and wasps swarmed all over the place. There were police and security – the black shirts and face-scanner goggles of the Home Security Office – surrounding the din, hemming it in. A robotic fire unit sprayed gallons of pink fire retardant onto the blaze.

She hid behind the fire unit and peered in at the burning mess. There was a big smoking crater where the Emerald Café had been. The surrounding buildings were a pile of burning rubble too – as if the entire block had been blown apart.

"Shit," she screamed.

She turned and fled, running down the long, slow steps, running from the explosion and the destruction, running in fear – fear for herself and Eileen and everything – running because she didn't know what else to do.

11.

The vision was nearly ready to go. It was to be uploaded to the Gorilla Information Network shortly after the cam-bots were secure and filming, releasing it as a live vision-stream immediately after some person was to arrive. Johnson couldn't quite follow what was going on between the snippets of information he heard, but he was excited to see the footage, whatever it showed about the Government retirement homes and his father's life. A small part of him held out hope that he may even see his father.

"With the cam-bots in place and the point-of-view camera that Parks has arranged, and now with your logins and the live DNA scan – which we will keep hidden from them – we can bypass Gorilla Industries' security and set up an online channel, so people can see what is truly going on," Camus explained.

Johnson edged closer to Camus' desk in the corner of the dusty humanist house. "Gorilla Industries is the biggest information provider out there too," added Johnson.

"Exactly," said Camus. "If we get it out on their information network, we can gain access to individual users across the world." He motioned to Johnson. "And because of your access codes and your position as an Information Editor, we can approve the content for the site, and then it will be uploaded and available to everyone with an internet connection. It will be searchable across the entire regulated internet." Camus grinned maniacally.

"And there won't be a thing they can do about it."

"But won't they be able to block it there too?" asked Parks.

"No, not really," Camus replied, his face becoming serious again. "Johnson's access will get it onto the network, which will get it out there so it's available across the RegNET. And then, even if they can work out its origin and try to take it down... ah, well, by then it will be unstoppable."

The Renegade glided over to the desk and slapped Camus jovially on the back. "That's great," he said.

"That's not all," said Camus. "We've designed it with an in-built virus to spread the content to the contacts of all those that see it. It will fly across the web from one computer to the next like wildfire."

"Good work, Camus. And Parks, what you - and your grandmother, of course - have done for the cause, well, we could never have done it without you." The Renegade paused. "We salute you both," he added with his hand across his heart.

"Thanks, Lenmar," Parks replied somewhat mournfully. "It's been the worst few weeks of my life. I just hope we get the footage up. For her!"

"And you too, Johnson," said the Renegade, "we couldn't have got here without you either."

Johnson felt a wave of anxiety. Despite their promises of security and safety, it was his logins and passwords they would be using. It was his thumbprints, and his live DNA scan - and surely they couldn't hide that. He took a deep breath. He was putting his life in the hands of strangers. He was making himself a target. But it also gave him a purpose. There seemed to be some fate in all of this, as if this was his destiny from the moment he had laid eyes on Maya at Gorilla Industries. But something niggled at him, drove into him like a splinter: if this was Maya's work, had she done everything – befriended him, dated him, fucked him, made him fall in love with her – for this? Did she want his passwords and logins all along?

The air seemed to thicken as they waited. Camus sat at the computer, busily typing and swiping the screen as he hooked up the live feed. Parks was on the other side of the room. She looked sullen, as always. She didn't speak. She held a Portable Internet Device in her hands, and stared at it, watching it with great intensity. She had yelled out a bit earlier, about them being in the truck and on the road – whatever that meant. Auntie Norma sat on a couch with a glass of whiskey, taking violent sips every few seconds, and the Renegade paced around the room in his black beret with the boot-print on the front.

Johnson was filled with nervous, almost fearful anticipation for what the footage of the retirement homes may show about his father and the conditions in which he lived. But Maya also remained at the front of his thoughts. Wherever she was, whatever her truth was, there was no denying that she had opened his eyes, taken him out of the compound walls of Gorilla Industries, and brought him to life. And there was their future he had to think about, which he had seen in his natural dream, and felt certain was real, like a memory not yet lived.

"That's it," said Camus, "all the cam-bots are in place."

The Renegade walked over to him and leaned over the screen. "Show me all the angles we've got."

"All the main rooms are covered: the entrance area, the waiting room and then the processing floors. We should be able to capture it all. Plus, if needed, the micro-lenses can reflect off water particles in the air, so we can pretty much see any spot we like, although those reflected shots won't be as clear as the direct images from the main cameras, and they only work over a short distance."

The Renegade rubbed his hands together excitedly. He asked Camus to pull the shots up, one by one, onto his main screen, and they began checking them, testing the cameras and lenses, and then the zoom and angles of each.

After the Renegade was satisfied with the cameras, he walked over to the corner of the room and stood facing the wall, his head moving around as he muttered to himself under his breath, like a boxer preparing himself for a title fight.

Eventually, Camus called Johnson over and offered him a chair, which had been rolled over to the desk especially for him. Camus attached a small, chip-like device to Johnson's finger; it went over the top so everything above the knuckle was covered by the grey plastic device, which was then hooked up to the LAN/S-pod. "Hold this," he said as he checked the attachments. "And don't let it fall off."

Johnson held the device firmly to his finger. He peered over at the computer screen with the images of the retirement home, trying to get a glimpse, but he couldn't see much beyond a sterile-looking warehouse painted green and white like a mint wrapper. He wondered where all the old folks were, and what it was they were trying to capture.

Auntie Norma's mouth hung open. She shook her head.

Parks was visibly upset too. "Disgraceful!" she said.

"What is it?" Johnson asked, almost jumping out of his seat to get a closer look.

"You'll see," Camus answered cryptically.

Johnson sat back down. He stared at the screen, his feet tapping on the ground impatiently. He saw nothing. He wondered what he was meant to be looking at. The others were motionless, engrossed in the vision. Johnson didn't want to ask further questions, and sat in silence, peering at the empty footage of the cold, green warehouse floor.

"She has arrived," said Parks as she rushed over to Camus and handed him her portable screen. "Here," she added. "Get it up on your screen."

Camus flicked on a second screen in front of him. Some dark footage appeared. "We can't see anything," he said.

"They're still in the truck. There's not much light. But it looks like they've stopped," said Parks. "The map is matching up with our bots on the floor."

Camus calmly leaned across Johnson, pulled the device and his finger in front of him, and pricked some blood through a hole in the side. Johnson felt the pin-prick and squirmed in his seat.

The Renegade bounded over. "Is it loading onto the Information Network? Have we got passed Gorilla security?

"Hold on, let me see," replied Camus as he tapped at the screen. He was quiet for a minute, then yelled out triumphantly, "Straight on! All security has been bypassed. We're in."

The Renegade cheered. "You little beauty, Johnson," he said.

Auntie Norma raised a glass. "That's the first step," she said. "And now for the rest... The main fucking course!"

Camus clicked a button, and vision of the empty warehouse reappeared on the main screen. "Do you want this image to start?"

"Yeah, let's get them coming in through the entrance," replied the Renegade. "Do you know where that will be?"

"It looks like there's a dock here, which we can zoom in on

from this camera," Camus said as he pointed at an image on the screen.

"The doors are opening," Parks said.

A door opened in the factory, and people slowly emerged. At first, it was just a few people stumbling forward into the warehouse, but then more and more of them came through, spreading across the floor like molasses.

"Cut to your grandma's eye," said the Renegade as he glanced at Parks. "I want us to get down amongst it." He put a hand on her shoulder. "She's a hero, what she's doing, you know."

"I know," Parks replied angrily. "She's my fucking grandmother." Then she ducked her head and walked away from the screens, facing away from everyone.

They all stared at Parks, and for a moment no one moved.

"We love her, Parks, for what she is doing... and we love you too," said the Renegade. "I god damn love you," he added.

Parks hesitated, swaying for a moment where she stood, before she acquiesced and sat down on the couch by Auntie Norma.

"Come on," said the Renegade. "Let's get back to it. Get the shot from her eye."

Some grainy vision appeared in a window. Camus enlarged it, and then tapped a few keys and the vision became clearer. The footage was from someone's point of view. They were in the crowd – they could see a pair of saggy dark-skinned arms in front, and a black-coloured blouse below, and people on all sides, crammed in for room, pushing up against one another. The point-of-view camera stopped. The camera swung around, surveying the gaggle of old folks before it. There were hundreds of them – all old, some feeble and hobbling, some walking along freely, others seemingly in a daze as they meandered forward.

"That's your grandmother?" Auntie Norma asked as she put an arm around Parks.

"That's her," said Parks. "But she wanted to do this," she added, and then hung her head between her legs, breathing heavily.

The Renegade was throwing out orders to Camus, making him cut between shots, taking footage from the 'grandma eye', as he called the vision from Parks' grandmother, and moving with it, zooming in on the other elderly people on the big, open factory floor.

"Get close on that man's face," bellowed the Renegade, and one of the cameras zoomed straight in on the eyes of an old decaying man, capturing a moment of fear and confusion. "Freeze on that. Great work, Camus," added the Renegade, before he was moving on to the next shot, and the next, sending the vision high up, like a bird, then down into the mess of people, capturing the sense of helplessness, confusion and concern within the room.

"They are moving through now," Camus said.

"Is there sound?" the Renegade asked. He stood behind Camus with his hands on his hips.

"Yeah, but it's not strong," Camus replied. "The microphone may be too far away to pick it up."

"We should have used a stronger one... and what about the grandma eye," he added as he looked over at Parks.

"What's that?" Parks replied, her eyes looking fierce as if she was going to attack him.

"I'll turn it up to maximum, and try to increase it from here," Camus said calmly as he played with the settings on the screen.

Suddenly, they could hear a muffled voice-over. It was directing the people on the floor to keep calm. "Please move down to the far end of the floor. Please line up in single file for your medical examination and psychometric testing – so we can match each of you with the appropriate retirement home."

Parks and Auntie Norma both swore. "What fucking bullshit," they said, almost in unison.

"Okay, cut to the next room," said the Renegade. "Let's get a little prelude to that."

Camus cut to a new room with white double doors at one end and a travelator up the middle.

"Let's get them coming along the travelator, hitting it from each side to build the suspense," said the Renegade, sounding like a film director. "We're still hooked into the GIN right?"

"Yes, the link is fine," Camus replied as he did a quick check of Johnson's finger, and then added another pinprick to keep the scan running. "Okay, did you want me to flick to the next room now?"

"That's what I said."

Camus followed the Renegade's heated instructions, and now the main-screen footage showed a processing plant with a travelator down the middle. The travelator, hemmed in by two glass sides topped with a black rubber railing, ran through a doorway and then made its way to various machines and robots with mechanical arms and other implements. They made a clunking sound while the travelator hissed along.

The doors opened, and now there was a lone figure moving along the track. He seemed unsure what was happening and held on grimly to both sides. He reached the first machine – a metal doorway – that sparked into life and shot glints of electric current all through him. His legs gave way and he collapsed with a thud.

Johnson screamed out, "What happened?"

"They stunned him," Parks replied.

The travelator continued, and Johnson watched as the man's limp body rolled over the end onto a lower conveyor belt and, in the process, flipped over. The man was then pushed into the centre, and held there by two metal wedges. His head was at the front now, about to plough straight into a barrier at the end. Johnson couldn't look. He turned away, a hollow, sickening feeling at the pit of his stomach.

Camus swore at some unknown God, and Johnson couldn't help but look back at the screen. The old man's head was now caught in a vice, which gripped him just above the eyes and held the man still while a giant mechanical arm swung around. It paused above the back of his head. There was a flash of red light and a sizzling sound.

"Zoom in on the mechanical arm," said the Renegade.

The camera shot closed in. At the end of the arm they could see a small white chip like a card protruding from the end. They all watched in horror as the card was inserted swiftly into the back of the old man's head.

"They are putting in a brain chip, I reckon. Testing it out while's he's still alive," said Auntie Norma. "Or scanning any data they can get from the poor bugger."

"They're mining the data for sure; getting every thought from his life and uploading it," added the Renegade as he scratched at his beard. "Plenty of money in data."

There was a bleeping sound from the electronic equipment that ran on the wall like a control board, and then the arm pulled itself away from the head, turning and re-inserting the chip into a section of the control board behind it.

"What the hell is happening?" Johnson yelled.

Auntie Norma stood up and walked over to him. "They are

harvesting his data, all his thoughts and memories, anything they can use."

"For the Brain Race," added the Renegade. "They will use the information on how the brain learns for use in artificial intelligence. And they will sell it off to the highest bidder, so they can keep working on developing a truly independent-thinking artificial brain."

Johnson was paralysed with shock. The travelator had turned the man's body to the side, and now it was moving slowly towards a hole in the wall, his head flopped to one side, with a thin trickle of bloody goo running along the conveyor belt behind him.

As the near-dead man exited, an enormous lady with long brown hair entered on the travelator from the waiting room. She screamed, as if sensing the crisis befalling her, but was hit by the electrified doorway mid-scream and collapsed silently to the floor.

"Quick, Camus," the Renegade shouted, his arms flailing about in front of him. "Get back to the main room and see if they heard that scream – maybe we can capture the horror of it."

"From the grandma eye," Camus suggested tentatively, using the touch screen to cut between cameras until he had Grandma's eye sharply in focus, then switching over to her with a heavy tap. She was now standing in line with the others, moving towards the doorway. They appeared not to have heard the scream as they plodded forward, oblivious, like a herd of deer making their way through a mountain pass.

Parks appeared by the computer again, watching the vision from her grandmother's point of view. She buried her head in her hands. "What have I done?" she said, anguish strewn across her face.

The Renegade put a hand on her shoulder. "She wanted to do this, remember, Parks. She did it so we can expose this killing for what it is – a systematic geronticide of our mums and dads. They should be our elders, but instead we wipe them out like an unwanted infestation..."

Then it hit Johnson – his father was in a retirement home too. He began to shake in violent waves. Camus saw what was happening and grabbed hold of his hand and steadied the device on his finger. "Don't let it drop," he warned. Auntie Norma held Johnson's back, to try to comfort him but also to keep him from falling to the floor.

"Is this a retirement–" Johnson began, but his words were cut off by the Renegade shouting out more orders to Camus, telling him to zoom in and out and capture the preferred retirees making their lonely way along the travelator, facing the electrified doorway and then meeting their fate with the brain chip, their limp bodies taking the final bend and heading off to another unknown room through a circular hole in the wall.

And now the Renegade focused in on Grandma's eye, trying to be there to capture her turn on the processing floor.

Parks' grandma seemed to sense her time had come, and as she reached the front of the queue, she calmly spoke to them all through the microphone in her eye. "My name is Gerineeda," she said in a quiet, unwavering voice. "I am a retiree. I was told I was being taken to a Government retirement home to live out my remaining days. But I have been brought here with this lot, other retirees just like me." She reached the doors, then went on: "Come, follow my journey, see where they are taking me, what they plan to do with me – a mother, grandmother, once an employee – too old and tired now to contribute to our *great* society.

Come see what they do with those of no use to the Economy, no use to them." She bowed her head and closed her eyes.

"Amen to that," said Parks as she watched her grandmother moving along the conveyor belt. She stared for a moment. "I love you, Gava," she added, then she kissed her fingers, tapped the screen playing the footage, and ran out of the room, not looking back to see her grandmother's brutal demise.

After her grandmother had been stunned, the eye camera faced upwards, towards the ceiling of the factory. All they could see were the pipes, painted white, and various air-conditioning ducts above as she moved along the travelator. The camera stopped with a jolt, shook for a moment, as a red light flashed, and then the vision coming from grandma's eye seemed to cut out and they were left with nothing but black.

"What's happened? Can you get us into the next room," said the Renegade. He rubbed furiously at the thick stubble on his chin. "Get on the other side," he bellowed.

"I can't, I can't," Camus answered. "We don't have a camera there."

"Well, why the fuck not?" shouted the Renegade.

"We only have them in the warehouse and the processing floor. I didn't know... but hang on, maybe we can reflect off the water particles, track a way down to what's happening to the bodies."

"Do it!"

Camus now worked furiously at the keyboard and the screen, like a child let loose on a new toy. They could barely follow his fingers as they flashed about, trying to get their last and final vision.

"What footage is going out on the internet?" the Renegade asked, onto his tasks now like never before. "Take them back to the processing floor while you sort out a shot. We have to keep people on it to the end."

What more can there be? Johnson wondered. This film he had helped them show to the world had become a brutal horror show worse than anything he'd seen on the holo-vision. He was sickened and beaten down – both at the same time – and he dared not think about his father.

Camus took their broadcast back to the processing room, where another old man was having his brain read by the mechanical chip-arm before departing through the hole, while yet another lady arrived at the electrified doorway for her stunning.

Johnson couldn't watch it any more. He stared down at his finger and the live DNA scan that was taking this footage out to the world, making sure it was seen by people across the Trade Bloc. All he could see in his mind was the face of his father, and the thought of him going through what he had just seen. He had to know. *Is this how it ended for all of them?* He looked up at Auntie Norma, still standing behind him. He wanted to break down and cry, but she squeezed his shoulders and whispered in his ear that they were nearly done, and to stay strong for Maya.

It didn't take Camus too long to get the final vision. He had somehow navigated the camera to reflect off the water particles in the air, so they could get a view beyond the hole in the wall – and he launched this as his next shot. All they could see was a huge circular pit, dark and lightless, and something on the edge dropping in.

"Zoom up so we can see in that pit," the Renegade commanded.

"We can't. That's as far as we can take it with a reflection," Camus answered, "and it is too dark in there anyway."

"What about one of our cam-bots. Can we move them into this room?"

"I don't know."

"Well, try it, damn it! We need to see it all. See what's going on down there."

Camus worked quickly. He pulled a joystick from the side of the computer, turned it on and began manoeuvring it about.

"Is it working?" the Renegade asked.

"Bot number three is moving. And I'm looking for an opening."

"Okay, okay. Good work."

"It looks like the only way is on the travelator, through the hole in the wall where they are sending the people, but then we might meet the same fate as the POV camera."

"Just go for it. And let's play straight from that camera, in case you get any sight of what happens in there."

"It's moving! We are on and going through," Camus said as the vision cut to the camera now moving along on the travelator, and through the low wall to the next room.

"Stay with it," ordered the Renegade.

Suddenly the camera footage was spinning, the white of the ceiling flicking around, through black, and then a tumbling orange light, growing in strength and size.

"It's falling," Camus clarified. "I'm increasing sound and strength."

The orange glow grew until it took up the entire camera. They could hear a sizzling sound, could almost feel the heat. Then it cut-out, and all that remained on the screen was total darkness, the absence of anything.

Camus was breathing heavily. The Renegade put his hands on Camus shoulder. "Our camera met the same fate as our elders.

A furnace, and falling into that heat, that flame, and then... nothing left but the remnants of their souls."

"Cremated," said Auntie Norma.

Everyone else was quiet now, registering all that they had seen. Camus sat at the computer, not even looking at the screen; he just stared blankly at the ground. "What the hell?" he said.

"That was hell alright," The Renegade added.

Auntie Norma's hands trembled, and she steadied herself by resting one hand on the desk. "How the fuck did it come to this," she said.

Johnson pulled the device off his finger. He walked out of the room and into the adjoining kitchen. He vomited into the sink. He stood up and vomited again, unable to control the retching. He wanted to vomit everything up, all his food and feelings, all his anger... all his essence. It was a cold, scaly lizard that sat in his oesophagus. He stood back and reached for a glass of water. He thought of his father, whom *he* had put into a Government retirement home... he had to know. He walked back to the main room.

"Do they–" he couldn't even say it. "Is that what happens with them all?" He looked first at Auntie Norma and then at the Renegade.

"Yes. That's what they do," Camus answered. "That's why we had to show it."

"My dad! My dad!" Johnson screamed.

The humanists all stared at him.

"I sent him there," Johnson spluttered, tears streaming down his face. "I killed him," he screamed.

Auntie Norma put a hand on his shoulder. "You didn't know. You couldn't know. No one does."

"It's not your fault," said the Renegade. "It's their fault – this whole damn system, where people are nothing more than the data in their heads, with every thought up for sale."

Johnson slumped onto the couch. He put his face in his hands and bawled. He had never bawled before; never felt tear after tear streaming down his face in an uncontrollable river of pain. He couldn't think; the words wouldn't come together in his mind. He was filled with unbearable sadness and overwhelming guilt. He didn't want to be alive. He wished he had never lived.

12.

The sun had set over the city and Johnson had spent the best part of the day marooned on the couch, lying in a puddle of despair. Camus had been on the computer for most of that time. They barely spoke. Parks had returned briefly. There was a short discussion between her and the Renegade, or Lenmar as they called him. 'A problem as arisen,' she said, before darting off and not returning.

Auntie Norma had come over to Johnson more than once, offering her support and a glass of water or whiskey. She made him a sandwich at one point, which he ate in heavy bites, barely tasting it. The Renegade came and went. He avoided eye contact with Johnson, as if he wasn't there, an insect unseen among the floorboards.

Johnson couldn't seem to see the group's sadness as they had seen his. He sensed their anger but wanted to connect with them more, to feel this moment with them. They had witnessed a horror together, yet, in a way, a river ran between them. They could never feel like he did. Only Parks could know what he had been through – she had seen it firsthand with her grandmother – but she had left and had not returned. The rest had known what was going on in the Government retirement homes; maybe not everything, or how it was done, but they knew of it. While Johnson had learned about it as he'd watched the live-stream, and thus faced the full impact and the despair of his father's gruesome fate.

He wished he'd never found out, never come here at all. It was too much for his body and mind to take. He almost craved the idea of being back at Gorilla Industries, editing blogs and web pages for the Network. And then none of this would have happened. He chose the wrong dream on his Dream Weaver, and it had turned nasty. He wanted out, to abort, before it was too late… but it was already too late. He couldn't change what he had seen. It was tattooed on his brain, etched forever in his psyche, as much a part of him now as his navel.

Not only was he dealing with grief for his father, the brutality of how it must have happened, and the unyielding belief that he was responsible, he also felt the pain of the millions of other lives lost on the conveyor belt of death.

Johnson was hollow, broken, and hardly human any more. He wanted to shout out to the gods of the past, to the elites of now – to blame someone for what he had seen. He wanted to run out of the house and grab hold of every person in the street, and scream of the horror he had witnessed. He wanted to flush himself into a stream, become one with the water and cease to be, like all those other poor souls, like Parks' grandmother, like the other men and women he'd seen on the film, like his father… the father who had always played with him and his brother when they were young; the father who had worked hard so they could have a roof over their heads and food on the table each night; the husband who had been cheated out of happiness by the death of his wife, turning to the bottle to cope, and then to his second son, Johnson, to help him in his time of need. And Johnson had sent him to his doom – on a truck to an abattoir, where he had been herded into a factory, stunned, with all his mind-data taken and sold to the highest bidder, his thoughts and memories saved on a chip to be used in the *Brain Race*.

The Renegade walked over to him. "How are you feeling?" he asked in a gentle voice.

"Not well. My father was in that home. I put him there."

"I know. But it's not your fault," said the Renegade as his eyes met Johnson's and he shook his head apologetically. "You didn't know. No one knew."

Johnson nodded. "Any news about Maya," he asked.

The Renegade sat down next to Johnson, almost touching. "Sadly, no. She is in what they call radio silence."

Johnson didn't follow.

"Uncontactable," clarified the Renegade.

"Do you think she's okay?"

"I don't know, but she is pretty capable..."

"She's not at Gorilla Industries?"

"We don't think so, but she could be there or anywhere really. It's hard to say."

Johnson felt deflated, the last gasps of hope hissing out of him like air in a blown bike tyre. "So what do we do now?"

"Well, Johnson, first of all, we need to leave this place," the Renegade answered. He rubbed the back of his hand against the bristles of his beard. "They're onto us. We just got word that one of our safe houses got taken out by Home Security hornets."

Johnson didn't know what to say. He sat quietly for a moment as the Renegade talked about some explosion at a café in the city. Eventually, Johnson asked if he could come with them.

The Renegade looked away, across the room. "It's not safe," he said. "You have to leave. Get out of here and go as far away as you can. Start a new life."

"But I don't have anywhere else to go," Johnson pleaded

The Renegade shook his head. "I am sorry it has to be this way."

Johnson felt a flood of wild, untamed energy course through him like a Pep-Me-Up pill. He jumped up and turned to face the Renegade head-on. "I am not leaving without Maya," he said sharply. "I came for her and I need to find her. I'm not going anywhere." Johnson stood, staring into the Renegade's powerful eyes. "I'll stay with you until we find her. Help you find her."

The Renegade paused and considered Johnson's proposition. "Alright, Johnson," he said, speaking in a slow, careful way. "You can come with us. Help us find Maya. That's your job, and we will help of course. But for now you have to get out of here. Find a safe house and hole up for a few days until we get ourselves set up again. We need to leave this place and make sure every trace of our presence here has been removed. And we can't risk you being here with us. Do you understand?"

"I guess," Johnson replied, not sure if he should feel left out, or proud that they would want to protect him like that. He sat down again. "Where will I find you then?"

The Renegade leaned in closer. "We will come for you the day after tomorrow."

Johnson felt a surge of relief. "Two days from now?

"That's right!" said the Renegade. "Camus, can you bring me some paper, so I can give Johnson the address."

Camus grunted and then felt around his desk until he found a notepad. He grabbed it, and a pen, and brought it over to the Renegade. "Here," he said, handing them over.

The Renegade wrote down an address, ripped the paper off

the pad and handed it to Johnson. "Be there on Wednesday at 15:00 sharp. Parks will come by and collect you in a white van. Make sure you are at that address at that time. Stand out the front and wait for the van. She will have all the details. Understood?"

Johnson nodded. "What do I do now?"

"Go home, Johnson. Be with your loved ones. Enjoy this life you have while you have it. And take a rest. You need it."

Johnson wondered where he could go for a couple of nights. It was late and he needed a place to sleep; a place to rest and recuperate, and to digest all that he had seen. There was only Conrad.

"Take this too," added Camus. He handed Johnson a small card.

"What is it?"

"A chip, so you can use the car-grid and buy things without your wrist chip," Camus replied.

For a moment Johnson didn't follow, until he saw the wound on his wrist where Parks had removed it. He took hold of the card with the built-in chip and put it in his pocket.

Camus gave Johnson the thumbs up and a nod, and then went back to his desk in the corner of the room.

Johnson hesitated, unsure how or when he was supposed to leave their hide-out. "Do you want me to go now?" he asked.

"It's best for you, Johnson," said the Renegade as he stood up. He tapped Johnson on the top of the shoulder. "Thanks, fella, for all you have done. Without you, we wouldn't have been able to upload the live-stream and tell the world the chilling truth of our retirement homes. People saw that footage, and it mattered. The truth always matters."

Johnson blushed as a wave of emotion rolled over him, a sense that he had done something important for the world. And even though that thing had broken him, it was something that needed to be shown. The people in Capital City and in the NABOJ Trade Bloc, and across the globe, needed to know. They needed to know the horrors that awaited those who had become superfluous to the Economy.

Johnson stood up. "I'd better get my bag," he said.

"We'll get that for you." The Renegade pulled out a blindfold from inside his jacket pocket. "And then Auntie Norma will take you back."

"Do I need to wear that again?" queried Johnson. He had done so much for them.

"I'm sorry, yes. We can't be too careful with these things."

Johnson felt the trust that had grown between them crumbling, like the last of the polar ice caps. He was just another person to them, not their brother. He stood, staring at the Renegade.

Auntie Norma returned with the green duffel bag filled with the last of Johnson's possessions. Johnson looked ruefully at the blindfold. "I'll tie it," she said.

"No way," Johnson stated firmly. "I'll go now myself, or you can take me, but I am not wearing that thing."

Auntie Norma looked at the Renegade, unsure what to do, and Johnson thought he caught a flash of anger in the man's eyes, but he spoke softly: "Okay, Johnson. You have earned that right." He turned to Auntie Norma. "Tint the windows."

Auntie Norma hesitated. "Are you sure, Lenmar?"

"Yeah. He is one of us now." And with those words, Johnson felt the joy of inclusion, of being part of something, of brotherhood. "It's time we moved on from this place anyway," added the Renegade. "Time for you to work your magic and create some new faces too."

As Johnson walked down the street, his hand searched around in his bag for his internet tablet. He couldn't find it, and eventually gave up the search and just walked on, head down. Auntie Norma had driven for what seemed like hours, and what felt like a series of concentric, never-ending circles, until they reached a desolate garage somewhere on the outskirts of the city. She had given him his bag, wished him well, and then immediately departed.

He took a hooded jumper from his bag and pulled it over his shirt as protection against the chilly wind that beat against him. He swayed one way and then the other, unsure how he should feel. He heard drones overhead. They scared him more than ever. *Are they looking for me already?* he wondered. He wasn't sure if he should believe Camus, who had told him that their hack would be clean and untraceable – not with them using his logins and DNA to get past Security. But at least, for now, they didn't know where he was.

He thought about the humanists, and what they had done together. He couldn't believe the way they had been portrayed – as anti-globalists hell-bent on destroying the Economy and all that everyone held dear. They were about the truth... whatever that was. He knew – from editing thousands of articles and blogs for Gorilla Industries – the truth could be whatever you wanted it to be. It didn't really matter what he thought, or what actually happened. It mattered what they thought – the corporations and their bought politicians, the elites and the property owners... and, sadly, the vast majority of workers and consumers who inadvertently supported a system that kept them trapped below, kept them housed in nothing more than battery cages.

But he had more to worry about than the inequalities of the

system. His father was dead. There was no denying the gruesome, frightful horror of what he had witnessed on that film. But Maya was alive, and she was his future, his one chance of escape, of happiness. Through her, he could pass on the torch of life – his life and that of his father.

He touched the piece of paper in his palm. He had held onto it with such force since leaving the house, he thought it may disintegrate. He looked at the address one more time. He would be there to meet Parks, and then he would do everything in his power to find Maya. It was madness to join their cause, he knew that, but it was also a chance to face his destiny, to be the hero, like the heroes he'd read about as a kid in the comic books his father had given to him – comic books his father had once received from his father before that, passed down through the ages, dust and all. And if he was that hero, then Maya would be his... and he could now see how their future ran together. For the first time it made perfect sense, as if he had needed to get to this place to truly know it.

It hurt, thinking about his father and, as he walked along, he tried to block it out; to block out the factory, the electric shock and data-mining, and his body ending in that pit of fire; to block out the horrible thought that he was more responsible for his father's death than anyone. He had stupidly made the mistake, seven years ago, to take him to a Government retirement home. He had willingly handed him over, signed the papers and waved goodbye – expecting him to be taken to a place of comfort, believing they could give him the food and shelter and medical attention that he needed. Instead, they had taken him away, stolen his brain, his thoughts, his humanity, and then expunged him from existence as if he'd never been.

Johnson wiped away his tears. He sat on a bench and threw his bag angrily to the ground. He took a few deep breaths and then bent forward, unzipped the bag and began to search more thoroughly for the tablet his father had given him. It wasn't there. *What happened to it?* he wondered. *Could I have lost it?* He thought back, but his bag had been with the humanists since his arrival at their house. The thought crossed his mind that they had taken it, but he didn't want to believe it. But without an internet device he was stuck.

At that moment, as if his desperate call had been heeded by the car-grid itself, a white car zoomed towards him. He held out his hand hopefully, desperate that its senses would pick him up. To his delight, it pulled over, only about fifty metres up the road. He ran towards it, and watched as a couple alighted. He sprinted desperately towards the car, shouting for it to remain, and then the woman saw him running with his bag, and held back for a second, keeping just enough of herself inside the car so it couldn't leave. "Thanks," he muttered breathlessly as he reached the car. She smiled and walked off. Johnson dived straight into the back seat, his bag landing with a thump beside him. The car immediately sensed his presence and demanded a new destination. He gave the autopilot Conrad's address. It was the only place he could go. He felt a little bad going back there so soon and endangering his friend. But it was only for two nights, and then he would join the humanists and find Maya.

The car flew off along the car-grid. Johnson looked out the window. The sky had darkened and the streetlights flickered into life. He saw block after block of skyscrapers and office buildings. They were like a canopy of trees, each fighting for light in the jungle mess. There were modern domes, red metal structures and entire walls of super-glass bathed in translucent colours – the colours and shapes of a city. He stared up at an office window, trying to make out the workers inside – sitting at their desks, humming away at their computers – but it was too dark and the window only reflected the streetlights. Cars moved in and out of the lanes at high speed, then shot off in different directions. Each block was more of the same: skyscrapers and office towers reaching for the heavens, covered in bubbled messages and company slogans, or grey and bland if a company wanted to remain anonymous and didn't need the revenue.

He looked out and counted the trees. There were only a few, dotted here and there along footpaths and squashed between buildings. Their time on earth was coming to an end as they were replaced by digital holograms and images that sang out from the screens crowding the cityscape – screens playing snippets of news headlines and endless hours of advertisements for toothpaste, Vitawater, the latest PIDs and Home Intelligence Units, beauty creams and everything in between.

13.

She pulled out her PID with its inbuilt internet phone, secured for this purpose, and dialled the number. A number she'd been given for emergencies only – but now was the time. Her hands trembled. Nothing happened. She hung up. She looked around the rubbish dump. It stretched on for acre after acre in all directions, with piles of bottles and junk and torn plastic bags spilling food-scraps and garbage across a thick carpet of endless rubbish, humped here and there into huge mountains as big as anything nature could produce. She felt safer amongst the forgotten trash, as if no one would bother to search for her out here, between the slums, where society's waste was dumped in hope that it may magically disappear altogether.

Once more, she dialled the number, which she had memorised for this moment. The phone rang. She steeled herself. Camus answered, stating his name curtly.

"Hi Camus. It's Una."

"Ahh, Una, how are you?" Camus replied.

"Good," she said. "Can you transfer me to Lenmar."

"Sure. Hold on." There was a pause, then the phone clicked and rang again. Someone answered it, but no one spoke.

"Lenmar, is that you?" she asked. "It's Una."

"Una Maya, well I never," he chuckled. "Where the hell have you been?"

"Around. I saw the Emerald Café get taken out by drones."

"Really? Fuck! Did they see you?"

"*Are you okay?* You mean," she shot back angrily.

"Sorry, yes. Well are you?"

"Sort of."

"Okay, good."

"Eileen is not, though."

"I know. Bless her soul," Lenmar said. He took a long, drawn-out breath. "You shouldn't be ringing. You know that. They could be tracing us."

"I know, but it's important. I'll be quick, I promise." She sounded weak, as she often did with Lenmar. She steadied herself.

"When are you coming back?" he asked. "We are leaving the house soon. We can get you from the restaurant, if that works?"

She ignored him. "Where's Johnson," she demanded.

"I don't know," replied Lenmar with a slight snigger, which he covered with a loud cough.

"I thought he was with you. That's what Parks told me. He helped with the live-stream, right?"

"Brutal, ha!"

"What, the footage? Yeah, awful. Poor Parks. She's a mess."

"Did you see her?"

She paused, kicking at an empty plastic bottle, and then denied contact. Lenmar was quiet. Una broke the silence: "Well, where is he?"

"I don't know. We dropped him at a garage in the city."

"Why did you do that?"

"He was too much of a risk to have around, you know that, Una."

"I specifically asked you not to let anything happen to him."

"And we didn't. We let him go..." Lenmar paused. "See, I'm a man of my word."

"If Gorilla Industries finds him, they will take him out."

"Yeah, well, I guess that's the way things are."

"Fuck you, Lenmar, the bullshit of a Renegade." Una felt the anger welling up inside of her. She kicked at a plastic bottle on the ground, then calmed herself and said: "Johnson's a person too. A person who helped us."

"And I want him to be okay, truly, to get away and start a new life or whatever... but he's not my responsibility. If you want to help him, then you help him."

"That's what I intend to do."

There was a pause. "What? Are you serious?"

"Dead serious," she said. "And I'm not coming back either." It felt good to say it.

"Come on, Una, we need you. You're our undercover star, the best we have, and you were a big part of our success with the homes."

She almost screamed down the phone that she regretted it all, but that would have been a lie. She had to admit that she loved what she did; it made her feel alive and gave her the chance to contribute to something bigger than herself, to help fight against the destruction of humanity.

Lenmar spoke on: "And we have other things we need to do, other projects."

Una had had enough. "I'm done," she said sternly.

"What do you mean, done?"

"What do you think I mean? I'm done, done with this shit."

"The shit is what drives you," Lenmar shot back, and then added: "Una, this is our way. We are exposing a failing system that has continued to treat people like livestock. We are spreading the truth to the people, fixing misinformation, providing the light in their darkness ... the last bastion of hope in a fading world."

"Save your speeches for the camera. There are other ways to help, to make a difference, and you can start by caring for everyone, not just the greater good; for actual people... individuals, and their lot in life, not just some grand idea of humanity."

Lenmar hesitated with his words. "You've got to come back. You won't find him."

"Yes I will. And I'll make sure he gets away from all this and has a good life. Now, I've got to go."

As Una went to hang up, she heard Lenmar shout at her through the phone, "I won't let you find him," and she knew then that she had to move quickly.

14.

Conrad opened the door to his house and walked inside. "Hey, Jay. How was your day?" he asked.

"I didn't do much," Johnson replied. He'd tried to sleep, lying in bed as the day went by, desperately searching for sleep; curled up into a ball, his eyes closed, his mind scattering from one thought to the next in a never-ending circle of madness. More than once, he had begged, implored, his brain to let him sleep, craving just one moment of unconsciousness. But his prayers, like most prayers, went unanswered.

"Wait a moment," said Conrad as he ducked into his bedroom.

Johnson stood, waiting, in the living room until he returned. Conrad grabbed two beers from the fridge, and they sat down, across from each other, on the couches. They sipped their beers in silence. They hadn't talked last night. Conrad had been ready for bed when Johnson arrived, tired and dishevelled. Conrad didn't ask any questions, which suited them both. Johnson didn't even know how to say the words to describe what he'd witnessed. And then he'd slept, slept right through the morning, missing Conrad when he left for work, not hearing a sound. He'd woken with a start and wondered for a moment where he was. And then everything came flooding back, and he hadn't wanted to stay awake any longer. So he had just stayed there in bed all day, trying to find solace in more sleep, which never came.

Johnson didn't mention the humanists. He knew how Conrad

felt about ecoterrorists and anti-globalists and it wasn't a fight worth having. Not now. Not as they sat together, enjoying each other's company for what could be the last time.

Conrad suggested they get some food. Johnson agreed. He suddenly felt very hungry. He hadn't eaten much all day, only getting out of bed a few times to pick his way through the kitchen, grabbing bread and biscuits and barely tasting them, wandering from the fridge to the pantry like a zombie, hardly knowing where anything was kept. He had wanted desperately to use Conrad's wall screen and to log on to his AppChat and About-Face accounts to see if Maya had messaged him, but he couldn't risk it from here. It would only expose his friend. And he couldn't do that, not after all Conrad had done for him.

As they drank their beers, he told Conrad about his father's death. Not how he died, but just that he knew, and that he'd been told. He couldn't face telling him what he'd seen on the live-stream, or saying it aloud, admitting he was part of it. He hoped Conrad would see the footage on the regulated internet, and it would wake him up from his own slumber and tacit support for the way things were. But, for now, he just wanted to talk about his father.

He stood up slowly, like he was rising to give a final eulogy for the old man. "My father wasn't perfect," he began, "but he raised me and my brother, Goliath. He loved us, and he made us laugh, and for a while there he really was a bright and special man – so caring and considerate. He always did his best to give us everything he could, no matter the circumstances. Like when Mum died. He stayed by her bedside day in, day out, barely leaving her alone for a moment. And it cost him his job, a job he loved. He worked for nearly his whole life, his whole working life for About U and then About-Face. And they showed their true colours... But he didn't give up. He worked on for as long as he could. He gave his best... to companies that put profit over people." Johnson felt the words of the humanists coming out of him. "In a system where companies don't give a damn about anyone but their shareholders."

"Steady on," Conrad interrupted, then, seeing the fierce look in Johnson's eyes, apologised and motioned with his hands for him to go on.

"Where companies forget that their employees – those who keep the whole thing going – are also sons and daughters and people beyond the four walls of their employee compounds." Johnson sighed. He rubbed his neck softly. "My father was a good man. And he is dead. They probably don't even remember him..." he said, trailing off. "But I do. I know what he did for me. He was my father. And I loved him."

Conrad sipped on his beer. "Your father was a good man, Jay," he said. "I remember going to your house when we were at school. He was always very welcoming and fun. Always had lots of games to play. He always had time for us. For you."

Johnson laughed as he remembered the ball games his father had made up when he and his brother were young. They were never bored then. His father had made life fun with nothing more than a brick wall and an old tennis ball.

"We should order that pizza you always get," Conrad suggested, "your father's pizza."

Johnson nodded. "Yeah, we should," he said, sadness in his eyes. He slumped back onto the couch.

Conrad spoke to Beth, his Home Intelligence Unit, and asked her to order the pizza. They were told they could expect it on a Mega-Menu bee within 11 minutes.

14.

"It's nice to sit here with you, you know and talk," Johnson said after a time.

"Yeah, it's great! I always love chatting about football and stuff with you, Jay. You're my boy," Conrad joked.

Johnson shook his head. "No, I mean really here with you, in this room. We should have done it more often."

"What, together?"

"Yeah, in the same place. Not over the AppChat, but right here." Johnson stood up. He looked across at his friend, his eyes watering, the emotion of the evening finally getting to him. "Give us a hug, man," he said.

Conrad hesitated. His head wobbled gently from side to side. The room was quiet. Then he got up slowly and embraced his friend awkwardly over the coffee table. Johnson felt a special connection to his old mate as they linked together, brothers in arms. It felt like they were school kids again, best friends staying at each other's houses, talking way past their bedtime while they gobbled down jelly beans, the words not mattering so much as the hours wasted in each other's company.

Conrad pulled away, using the opportunity to go to the fridge to get two more beers. As he sat back down, Conrad asked his friend when he was leaving.

"Tomorrow," Johnson assured him. It felt as if Conrad wanted to get rid of him. And who could blame him? "If anyone ever asks, tell them that I threatened you, forced you to let me stay on pain of death," Johnson added with a laugh.

Conrad gave him a strange look and then burst out laughing. "You couldn't threaten a fly, Jay."

15.

Johnson packed up his clothes, unsure if he would ever return. There was a hint of nostalgia in the air as he zipped up his green duffel bag and hoisted it over his shoulder. He'd enjoyed seeing Conrad, having a last breakfast together on his tiny porch, eating warm, crusty bread and goat's cheese, and even an avocado that Conrad had somehow managed to procure – it almost felt like his last supper.

After Conrad had cleared the table and had gone to find the cleaning-bot, Johnson had sat out in the morning air, thinking about the decisions that had led him there. He'd looked up at a small brown bird perched on a nearby roof and watched as it fluttered its wings and launched its delicate body into the air. An eerie calm had descended upon him. And it was then that he knew he was right where he ought to be. Fate had taken him along; he had joined in its chorus and chosen a path, this path, for love. He would go out there and find Maya, and then never come back to this life, never be a part of the wheel again, never allow it to turn like it did, day after day, Monday to Saturday and then back again, churning up people and bodies like a combine harvester. And as he'd watched the bird sail high in the air, above the porch and the city, he'd let it all go...

He walked to the door with Conrad. He shook his hand and then pulled him in for another hug as they said their goodbyes on the doorstep of his home.

"Are you sure you want to go?" Conrad asked.

Johnson was scared, but he knew he had no choice. "I need to find Maya," was all he said.

Conrad just shook his head. "Well, I can't really discourage that, not after I encouraged you to chase her in the first place," he chuckled. "Be careful, mate," he added seriously.

Johnson smiled. "I will, brother," he replied. He was just glad that he'd been able to spend time with his old school chum, his one true friend.

Conrad wished Johnson luck as he edged back inside his house. "Let me know how it goes," he added.

"Sure. Thanks for letting me stay, Conrad, for the second time. It is much appreciated. You're a good man," Johnson said as he headed away from the house.

"You too, Jay. Now I've got to get to work. I'm already late." Conrad waved one more time, then, just as he was closing the door, Johnson yelled out for him to stop. Conrad paused.

Johnson thought about walking back inside and telling him everything, but he couldn't face it, couldn't face the questions or the explanation. Instead, he stayed where he was and shouted out, not caring who heard: "There's something I need to tell you." He paused, and then spoke on hurriedly: "They are killing the elderly... like my dad. He was murdered by the State."

Conrad hesitated. "What's that?" he asked, his voice quivering slightly.

"They killed him," Johnson yelled.

"What do you mean?" Conrad shouted back.

"Go onto the RegNET, any network. Go see for yourself. There's footage from one of the Government-run retirement homes here in Capital City. They are killing the retirees who don't have enough money to support themselves, using them for data."

Conrad stood in shock. Johnson thought he saw him trembling. "That's what happened to my dad," Johnson added. "Now I am going but promise me that you will watch it. You need to see that horrible fucking footage. You need to see it all."

And with that, Johnson was gone – up the street, at rapid pace, not looking back at his friend, who he could sense was still in the doorway, staring in disbelief.

As Johnson rounded the corner, he heard a police siren in the distance. He wondered where it was headed, and if it had traced him to Conrad and was coming for them both. He pulled the hood up on his jumper and began to jog.

He headed to the train station, feeling alone and scared – he had no job, no family, no way of even connecting to the internet, nowhere to go but the address he'd been given by the humanists. And he had some time to kill before the meet-up with Parks. He needed to get off the street too. He decided, on a whim, to go back to the Botanical Gardens and spend some time in one of the last remnants of nature within the district walls, in a place he had been before with Maya, a place that felt safe.

16.

Una traipsed through the Millennium Museum, retracing the same steps she'd taken with him only a few weeks earlier, seeking him out, popping into every room, her eyes flickering to each corner, behind the displays, under tables, everywhere. *It must look suspicious,* she thought. But for once she didn't care.

She was worried that she may be searching for a ghost... but within that fear, there was also hope, and hope drove her onward; hope that she could do something to help him in his hour of need.

Una had no idea what she was doing, or where to look. If she had access to Camus, she'd ask him to search through Johnson's social media posts, trace his friends and find him that way. But she couldn't and it left her feeling helpless.

Johnson had never replied to her messages - not the one about meeting at the Emerald Café or her follows ups, which had been more carefully worded with the fear that it was her message that had attracted the Home Security Office to Eileen. The messages had never even been seen according to the messenger app - which was a worry. But then, she knew he had ditched his Eye-Tab back when he deserted Gorilla Industries. She craved a sign, and yelled out to the air in her moments of panic, pleading for him to find another way to log-in, to communicate. She took a breath, calmed herself, knowing that maybe he was avoiding this out of necessity: aware that any online activity was traceable, knowing the risk it posed to his safety and liberty. But now, since the release of the retirement home footage, those risks had been magnified a thousand times.

She knew he was in mortal danger. And what hope had he now that he had served his purpose and the Humanists had abandoned him as well.

He could be anywhere, she thought. *He could have been arrested or taken out.* But she looked anyway, retracing the same steps they took the last time they saw each other.

She walked towards the Botanical Gardens; found the spot on the grass where they had lunch only a few weeks earlier. Her eyes darted about uncontrollably, almost seeing him at every turn, and then running forward enthusiastically, only to realise it was not him at all – didn't even look like him; it was just her mind making him appear everywhere.

She sped up, moving around the gardens in concentric circles, going back the way she came, desperation in every move.

17.

He bought some takeaway pasta and ate it by the rose garden. He savoured each bite. Lunch had never tasted so good. He knew it was the moment that was affecting his judgement, but all his senses seemed heightened.

He lay on the grass, staring at the sky. He looked at the advertisements that covered the heavens with their bright colours and logos. The blue and red of About-Face, the green bubbly AppChat, the black and white of Amazon Global, the dark blue of Anglo-American Finance, the pink of P2, the grey apple painted to resemble a cloud, the big yellow M, the fierce banana-smiling gorilla that flooded him with anger, the Lylo top hat, and his namesake, Johnson Goliath, splashed forever in the skies above in brown block letters, reminding him of the origin of his name.

He gazed at the hundreds of different advertisements, placed in orbit above, casting great shadows across the earth when the sun rose above them. As he contemplated them, he wondered about the world beyond the advertisements - the universe out there with the sun and the stars and the planets, and great solar systems of infinite size. He was so small - merely a dot on the great landmass of the earth - and even this vast planet was tiny and insignificant in the grand scheme of things. Yet here he was, lying on the grass, feeling the earth on his back, surrounded by trees and plants that grew in all directions; little insects that buzzed around him in hyperactive spasms; and ants plodding along in columns in search of communal food, like infantrymen on the march. He was connected to it all – one consciousness with everything that lived and had ever lived. He felt enormous yet infinitely small, his body an encasement for the vastness of his essence, yet an anatomic part of the essence of all, as much a part of the gardens that surrounded him as the great stars scattered out across the universe.

He got up and traversed the grounds of the gardens, stumbling along its weaving paths, under the tropical palms and ancient figs. He came to the succulent garden and its myriad of eccentric plants. He thought of his day here with Maya – that perfect day among the plants – and the magic that it had unleashed in him.

When it came time to leave, he felt sad at having to go. There was the risk that he might not come back, and he may never see such beauty again. But it had to be done. Maya was his future. He had gambled everything on her. She was out there, and this was his one chance to save her. And when he found her, they would head off, out past the slums, and set up a house somewhere. Start over, grow some vegetables, and raise some chickens and then have a child. He knew it – he'd seen it in his dream. And that dream drove him on, ever on; and drove him now across the grassy fields of the Botanical Gardens.

He stopped momentarily at a bin to drop off his rubbish bag containing the remnants of his pasta. Then he hopped on another driverless car running on the car-grid, using his disposable chip to pay the fare. He checked the car-clock – saw he had some time – and alighted a few blocks from the address that the Renegade had given him for the meet-up with Parks. He thought it might be better to walk the last two blocks, in case his movements were being traced.

He walked slowly; he still had about 15 minutes until he was meant to be at the meeting place. He stopped and leaned against a wall, briefly basking in the sun, before heading on again. He turned left down one of the streets and headed to the next corner, where he'd been instructed to wait. He looked at the street signs. He was in the right place. He paced around for a few minutes, looking up and down the street for the white van he'd been told to expect.

A drone suddenly dropped down from the sky and hovered about 20 metres in front of him. It turned and faced him, its camera eye trained on him, checking him against the facial recognition database. He would already be on a State watchlist if Gorilla Industries had sent his profile to the Home Security Office. Johnson stood there frozen, unable to move. He trembled with fear. *It is going to shoot,* he thought. He could feel it lining him up in its sights. This was his end. But then suddenly it flew off, darting down an alley in search of other prey.

He breathed out heavily. He was in danger, he knew it. He could feel the world closing in. What was he doing?

The white van was heading down the street. He could see it clearly now. It was one block away, driving slowly. He tried to look through the windscreen. It was tinted. *Parks must be in there,* he thought. He waved, trying to glimpse the figure inside.

The van slowed down. It approached him carefully, came right by him, then edged forward beyond where he stood. The van had a thin blue line painted down one side. He moved forward, ready to jump in the back. This was his moment.

Suddenly, the doors flew open. Four State Police soldiers jumped out, dressed in dark-blue puffed-up bulletproof vests with matching helmets and boots. They were on him before he could say a word, before he could even think.

He was wrenched brutally to the ground. A heavy knee slammed into his back, causing it to spasm. He screamed out. His bag was ripped from him and thrown away. Panic overwhelmed him.

"Do NOT move or we will shoot," said one of the soldiers. He was scared for his life, for his safety, for everything. But he couldn't move, even if he wanted to – the police soldiers had hold of him with the strength of a dozen bears. *What happened?* he wondered, before his head was pushed into the pavement, his face and eye mashed into the hard concrete surface.

They cuffed him tightly. He shrieked out in pain. He looked up to see a machine gun aimed at his face. The police soldiers picked him off the ground with ease and dragged him towards the van. He tried briefly to resist, digging into the ground with his feet, but a heavy punch thudded into the back of his head.

PART IV

1.

He takes hold of the tray and scans his wrist on the serving-bot. He can just make out the scar where the wrist chip had been removed. It is now almost covered by the barcode that had been tattooed down the inside of his arm when he first arrived.

He watches as the infra-red light flickers over his barcode and the tray is released. He walks over to a table and sits down. He looks around the cafeteria. It reminds him a little of the Gorilla Industries cafeteria, except that he doesn't get a choice of food here. He has to accept what the serving-bot gives him. That, or not eat. He looks down at the white synthetic plate sitting proudly on the contrasting red tray. The plate is half-covered with Beefo pie and a big dollop of some unknown sauce. There is a small pile of squished salad in a cup on the side.

He has tablets too, like he did in the old days, but he keeps them in his room for when he needs them most. There is a sleeping pill, a multivitamin – which is especially important, as vegetables are limited and he rarely sees the sun – and a sedative, which he uses during anxiety attacks, and which seems to keep most of the inmates in a perpetual daze, calm and tranquil, without the need for violence.

He thinks about Maya a lot, about those intoxicating weeks when she was all that mattered. *Was it worth it?* he often wonders. He would still be at Gorilla Industries now if she'd never come into his life. But would that be much different to his current life? He still works nearly every day, but now he works for the prison. It's a similar job too. They knew he was an Information Editor on the outside, and now they get him to use those same skills for them, redacting online information and blogs that mention the prison, Globohold, or any part of the punitive judicial system.

It's easy enough, although he finds it difficult to say anything good about the prison or the judicial system. It is almost farcical to suggest there is a judicial system or any way of obtaining justice. He has been locked up without a trial since he arrived. They won't even tell him the charge or why he was arrested. He knows, of course, but he hasn't heard anything from anyone. There's been nothing official. Nothing since the day the police nabbed him on the street and threw him into the back of a van like a juiced-up chicken. He was taken to a holding cell for the night, where they performed a DNA swab and took his fingerprints, and then they'd brought him in here, and given him a small cell and some clothes, while a brief run-down of the prison was played to him from the television set in the corner of his cell.

Two days he'd been given to grieve his loss of freedom, and his loss of Maya, which he'd spent lying, prostrate, on the hard bed in his cell. And then he'd started working as an Information Editor for Globohold.

They don't know about Maya, of course, and it's as if he buried her, and any hope of seeing her, upon his arrival at the lock-up, his home now for the next... however long.

He munches slowly on the chunks of beefo and pastry in his pie. Must be cheap. It doesn't taste of much. It's just texture in his mouth, with carbohydrates to give him the energy to get through another evening. He watches as the last inmates come through the cafeteria and order their dinners. Only the stragglers and broken-limbed lumber in through the cafeteria doors this late – big, tired men in blue overalls if they work outside growing vegetables, or in chequered shirts if they work in the robotics wing. There are other units too, hired out to companies needing cheap labour to build roads and other necessities, or working late in the prison factory, manufacturing products sold online by Globohold, and little plastic fridge magnets for the gift shop on prison tours.

It is the prison tours where he sees his chance of escape. It may be his only chance – and it's a small one. It's likely he will barely make it outside before he is blown away by a guard. But he counts down the days, the 100 days he has given himself, which he notches into his cell wall each night, secretly hoping that he doesn't have to go through with it, that his case comes before the courts or he hears from Conrad, or one of the humanists shows up in here with a way to get him out. But those things seem more fanciful each day, and each day brings him closer to 100. And as he gets closer to his deadline, he has begun to think about extending it out to 200 days or longer.

Johnson wears a grey shirt around the prison. It is barely any different to the shirts he wore at Gorilla Industries for nine years. But at least then he got paid, even if the deductions for his home unit, internet access and other costs had taken away most of his weekly pay packet. Here he works for credit, which can only be used at the prison store or in the cafeteria. It's too bad if it can't be spent. "Use it or lose it," they say, but there's only so much to use it on: cafeteria food; treats like coffee and chocolate; extra medication or tablets; a few hours locked into a virtual reality simulation or hooked up to the web playing an online sports game; or his favourite – a dream on the Dream Weaver, but they are limited to one a week. He can gamble with the other inmates as well, but they are all gambling with what they have too much of: prison credit.

He walks despondently out of the cafeteria, passing the robo-guard that mans the entrance. He saw the robo-guard move once – to break up a fight – it moved like a leopard and in a matter of seconds had put both antagonists to sleep with a tranquiliser gun. It reminds him of the owl at Gorilla Industries. But he has gotten used to mechanical guards now that he's in jail; there are robots stationed in every room and outside every cell, ready to pounce on any misbehaviour spotted by the camera systems that watch every inch of the prison grounds. There are a few real-life guards as well – humans making a living in the private prison system. But the robo-guards cost less and are 'programmed to act with no possibility of error'.

The world outside feels nearly as foreign to Johnson as the slums did in the days when he lived in the Employee Village. The same cannot be said for those outside of the prison walls. They can catch a close-up of Johnson and the other inmates on their holo-visions any time of day, on the prison channel, which shows continuous, 24-hour live action from inside the private prisons across the Trade Bloc. Everything the cameras record can be beamed out across the internet as part of a joint revenue stream for Globohold and Incarcer8 Ltd – the main rivals in the fight for prison supremacy.

Johnson walks along the corridor. He hears a hideous scream coming from one end. *It must be coming from the chamber,* he thinks. There are always screams and odd sounds emanating from that cold, closed-off room at the far end of the corridor. There's a rumour that they do experiments in there – testing new drugs, artificial brain implants or anything with significant risk – paid for by companies desperate to test their latest products on real people before they can be launched onto the market. And the pharmaceutical and technology giants come directly to the private prisons, which, it seems, are happy to oblige for the right fee.

Johnson scurries past the last robo-guard before his cell. It is his daily marker when walking along the corridor. It looks the same as all the other robo-guards, but there are a few subtle differences to the trained eye – mainly around the polish of the metal and some scratches in the paint. He can always tell *his* guard, just as the friends of identical twins can always tell them apart.

The cell door opens. He walks through. The door closes automatically behind him. The roof is fitted with a scanner that knows his exact dimensions. It will only open for him or his identical replica, as well as any of the robo-guards of course.

"Prisoner A5CD-27144Y secured and locked down," he hears from the automated voice-over of the prison security system. He struggled to adapt to being called a letter-and-number sequence when he first arrived, as if this was the final nail in the coffin for his identity. But he is used to it now, and knows the sequence by heart. He is Prisoner A5CD-27144Y.

Johnson Goliath, the company, hadn't been happy, and they sent a communication to him, care of the jail, requesting payment for breach of contract. Its legal team had advised that because he wasn't called Johnson anymore – and Johnson Goliath had paid out his parents for the use of his name for the rest of his natural life – it had a right to restitution. Johnson Goliath had worked out an amount they claimed represented 'fair and reasonable compensation for severance of the contract', or he could go back to being called Johnson. An in-house counsellor confirmed the worst: he would remain Prisoner A5CD-27144Y and, due to a pre-existing agreement between the private prisons and the debt companies, he would need to pay Johnson Goliath the full value of the debt before he could ever be released.

He lies down on his bed. His back aches. It is steadily getting worse. It has been playing up since his arrest, since the sharp wrench inflicted by the police soldiers as they took him to the ground. The poor-quality beds don't help either – a thin, slippery mattress on the hard, bubbly yellow concrete of his cell.

He looks up at the ceiling. He wants to turn off the lights and close his eyes, but he doesn't have any control over the lighting system. When the automated prison system turns off the lights, it turns them off for everyone. He waits, covering his eyes with his bed sheet. He thinks about his father, pained as he always is by the terrible truth of his end. He sometimes wonders why they haven't done the same to him – but they probably realise he's still got some use left in him as an in-house jail editor.

He grabs his remote and turns on the television bolted on to a corner of the cell. It's no holo-vision. They can only access the shared HV in the common room. He misses his couch and the giant wall-sized HV screen in his home unit, and he is still getting used to squinting to see the action on the small screen. He was told during the online welcome video that the television sets were graciously donated to the prison by a now-defunct television company – and although they are small, it is better than before, when the inmates had nothing to watch but the four yellow walls of their cells.

The Newslink nightly news is on. He still likes watching

the news. It connects him to the world outside the prison walls. There is a beacon of hope in remaining connected; knowing what is going on out there, in case his matter is ever heard by one of Capital City Court's robo-magistrates.

There is footage on the screen of smoke emanating from a building. The narrator speaks over the pictures in foreboding tones: "We bring you news from a recent anti-globalist attack on The Data Collection Bureau."

Johnson sits up, intrigued, as always, by the anti-globalists.

The narrator goes on: "This is the third attack this week. And authorities believe it is connected to the release of the fake 'retirement home' film – which has now been analysed by multiple authorities and proven fake, and the work of a disgruntled Gorilla Industries employee."

Johnson jumps out of bed. He feels a pang of anger rush through him – knowing they are talking about him, and trying to discredit the footage he knows to be true. He stands up on the bed, trying to get as close to the screen as possible. He turns up the volume.

"We have some CCTV footage of the perpetrators of the latest attack escaping from the Data Collection Bureau, which we will be showing now. If you recognise any of these people, please contact your local police, or the Home Security Office through its web page. A link has been provided below."

Johnson sees three figures scurrying out of a building, through a maze of alleys and over a brick wall. There is something about the way two of them run; he knows their gait or the way they hold their bodies. The camera zooms in. He stands up on his bed, trying to get as close as possible to the little television screen above. *Is that them?*

The narrator speaks: "We have images of the attackers." The image cuts to a photo, their faces frozen in time, captured by a camera during their daring escape. They look different, their faces have changed, but there's also a similarity that concerns him. *Is it really them?* he wonders. *Parks and Camus, with a dark-haired stranger?* If so, they are on the outside, free, causing mayhem on the streets... and not in prison, like he is. He swears, punches at the wall, furious that he is the one copping the punishment for their collective actions.

He flops down on his bed. He whimpers, unable to understand why he is in prison and none of the others are. *At least Parks should have been caught,* he thinks. It was her van he was supposed to be meeting that day. He doesn't want to think about it. It makes him mad with rage. Maybe he's imagining the similarity, and it's all in his head. He wonders if he should take his mind off it by ordering a night with the Dream Weaver... use the same dream he always gets – Maya!

The thought of her name shakes him up, reminds him of what he has just seen. There is something familiar about the stranger too – a blurred photo of a girl with dark hair and olive-brown skin.

The camera zooms in on a photo of all three attackers, moving across each face until it reaches hers. She has a different chin, thinner cheeks and longer hair – but her eyes are the same – big chocolate-brown eyes that stare out from the photo, reminding him of their night together, when she had stared into his eyes and made him fall in love with her.

UTOPIA / DYSTOPIA

Utopia / Dystopia is made up of The Information Editor (Book 1), and *The Storyteller* (Book 2). The books are written as two halves of the same whole - but opposites in every way.

THE STORY TELLER

Emerald and her community live off-grid — rejecting a Government that has failed the people, trying to be the change necessary to save the planet. They also take Ayahuasca in special ceremonies, which binds them together in their search for a better way. All that is missing is her daughter, Esme.

Their life is thrown upside down when The Lost Revenue Service comes looking for much needed tax dollars. But who sent them? Will it bring Esme home? And can Darcy, a fast-talking city lawyer, rescue them or will his efforts end up destroying everything they hold dear.

The Storyteller was written as a utopian vision of the world and as a counter to the dystopian novel, *The Information Editor*. The stories are written as opposites — two halves of the same whole, with hope and despair in equal measures. They are about our collective journey. But also, the importance of every individual life within that journey.

UTOPIA/DYSTOPIA
THE STORY TELLER
MILES HUNT

ABOUT THE AUTHOR

Miles Hunt was born in 1982. He is the author of *The Unfortunate Death of James Douglas O'Flaherty*, which was published by ASP in 2017, *The Information Editor* (2021) and and *The Storyteller* (2025). This work should be read as part of the *Utopia / Dystopia* duology. Miles is a failed lawyer, comedian, and political activist. His writing is informed by his love for satire, philosophy, and the constant search for experience. He lives in Sydney with family and pet cat and his favourite colour remains orange.

www.ingramcontent.com/pod-product-compliance
Ingram Content Group Australia Pty Ltd
76 Discovery Rd, Dandenong South VIC 3175, AU
AUHW020133130726
429791AU00001B/14

9 781763 788824